Martin Schongauer

NORTHERN EUROPEAN ENGRAVERS OF THE FIFTEENTH CENTURY

Martin Schongauer, Charles Ilsley Minott
Master LCz and Master WB, Alan Shestack
The Master of the Housebook, Jane C. Hutchison

CHARLES ILSLEY MINOTT

Martin Schongauer

Collectors Editions   NEW YORK

The author and the publisher thank the following institutions for permission to reproduce the illustrations:

Basel, Oeffentliche Kunstsammlung, figs. 9, 15; Berlin, Gemäldegalerie der Staatlichen Museen, fig. 7; Boston, Isabella Stewart Gardner Museum, fig. 3; Brussels, A.C.L., fig. 13; Colmar, Musée Unterlinden, figs. 2, 4, 5; Frankfurt, Städelsches Kunstinstitut, fig. 10; Munich, Alte Pinakothek, figs. 1, 6; New York, The Metropolitan Museum of Art, fig. 11; New York, The Pierpont Morgan Library, fig. 14; Philadelphia, John G. Johnson Collection, fig. 12; Vienna, Kunsthistorisches Museum, fig. 8; Washington, D.C., National Gallery of Art, Rosenwald Collection, fig. 16.

In memory of
James L. Minott

Contents

LIST OF FIGURES

Introduction

THIS study has been written to supplement the reprinting of Max Lehrs' *Geschichte und kritischer Katalog des deutschen, niederländischen und französischen Kupferstichs im XV. Jahrhundert*. It is primarily intended as a discussion of the present state of our knowledge about the German painter and engraver, Martin Schongauer. The discussion is in four chapters.

The first, biographical chapter, presents the conclusions of most recent interpretation of the documents and other evidence available concerning the major aspects of the artist's life. The information available, however, is far from complete and has often been interpreted in differing ways. For that reason there has been much controversy about the probable birth-date and the chronology of Martin Schongauer's career. The two major contributors to Schongauer scholarship in recent years, Eduard Flechsig and Julius Baum, substantially agree with the position taken by Lehrs, that the artist was born about 1450 and that his productive career must have spanned the years from about 1470 until his death in 1491. But the alternative argument, that Schongauer was born about 1430 or even earlier than that, has been held by many equally distinguished scholars.

The second chapter is a discussion of Martin Schongauer as a painter. Here the controversy becomes important. If the artist's career was limited to the relatively brief span from approximately 1470 until 1491 then the fruitless search for attributable works that date between around 1450 and 1470 can be dropped and the close stylistic affinity between all his known works is more readily understood. Moreover, this concept places a significantly different interpretation on the relationship of Martin Schongauer's art to its Netherlandish and earlier German sources.

The same problems apply to Martin Schongauer's engravings which are the subject of the third chapter. These are discussed in the general sequence of the Lehrs *Katalog* rather than chronologically, partly to correspond to the work at hand, but primarily because the juxtaposition of similar subjects from differing periods in an artist's life often serves as a

more explicit demonstration of his development. The chronology of Schongauer's major engravings is not particularly problematic. The evidence for dating them, in fact, supports the modern interpretation of the chronology of the artist's life. For the most part, however, it is impossible to place a precise date on the individual prints. The general phases of Schongauer's development in engraving may be summarized as follows.

Clearly, the eleven prints signed with a vertically stemmed "M" in Schongauer's monogram are his first works. All of them probably date before 1475. The major prints in this group are the four engravings in the so-called "Life of the Virgin" series, L.5, 6, 7, and 15, plus the large *Tribulations of St. Anthony*, L.54. The works of Schongauer's early maturity, probably dating between 1475 and 1480, include his most ambitious projects, from the huge *Christ Carrying the Cross*, L.9, to the twelve engravings of Christ's Passion, L.19–30. With the development of Martin Schongauer's mature style, through the 1480's, the evolution of his art is much more subtle, marked by a reduction in detail and a surer hand. There is a bolder sense of graphic design, volume, and space. The *Nativity*, L.4, *Baptism of Christ*, L.8, *Christ Appearing to Mary Magdalene*, L.15, *Christ Crowning the Virgin*, L.17, and *Christ Blessing the Virgin*, L.18, are among the best of Schongauer's works in this period. There is little point in speaking of late works by Martin Schongauer. His art, because of his early death, certainly never realized its full potential. Some evidence that his style was still evolving can be seen in the two engravings forming the *Annunciation*, L.2 and 3, which must stand among his last works. The volume of the figures is more positive, the indication of movement more subtle and graceful than the previous works.

In a short concluding chapter, the most important recent studies of Martin Schongauer's art are discussed and the interpretation of his contribution is summarized. The intricate problems of connoisseurship connected with Martin Schongauer's drawings are beyond the scope of this book and have been exhaustively treated elsewhere.

The Life of Martin Schongauer

MARTIN Schongauer lived and worked in the Alsatian town of Colmar for most of his active career. Though he was trained and productive as a painter, it was primarily through his engravings that Schongauer's fame and influence spread, even during his own lifetime. His productive years, according to most modern scholars, spanned the period from just prior to 1470 until his death in 1491. Nevertheless, the information that has been pieced together from various archival documents and other contemporary records to form an account of Martin Schongauer's life is by no means complete and is subject to differing interpretations.[1]

Martin Schongauer was one of several sons born to Caspar Schongauer, a goldsmith and member of an old distinguished Augsburg family. Caspar Schongauer settled in Colmar about 1440. He was the son of an Augsburg merchant, also named Caspar; grandson of one Hans Schongauer; and great-grandson of Konrat Schongauer whose name appears in an Augsburg document of 1370 as a master of the weavers' guild. The family was probably descended from Heinrich Schongauer (Hainricus de Schongowen) who was an Augsburg city-administrator (*Stadtspfleger*) in the second half of the thirteenth century.[2]

Caspar Schongauer, the goldsmith, was enrolled as a citizen (*factus civis*) of Colmar in 1445, and in the same year became a member of the town-council.[3] The document establishing Caspar Schongauer's citizenship rights gives his address "uff Fridolin Harneschers hus in der Schedelgassen." This refers to a house known as the "Haus zum Gatter" owned by Friderich Bennfelt, a harness maker. Later, perhaps by 1450, Caspar Schongauer purchased a house on the same street from one Burkart Giger, known as the "Haus zum Geige." In one of these houses, more probably the latter, it is likely that

Martin Schongauer was born. Nearby, in the same street, was the house of Caspar Isenmann, the painter to whom the youth was probably apprenticed. Although no record of Caspar Schongauer's birth, apprenticeship, or admission to the smiths' guild seems to have survived, it is now generally concluded that he served his apprenticeship in Colmar and became a guild member there in the early 1440's. If so, it is likely that his marriage took place at the same time, although that record is also unknown.

Caspar Schongauer and his wife Gertrude had at least four, and probably five, sons. Georg and Paul became goldsmiths, and there seems to have been a third son, Caspar, who also followed his father's craft. Ludwig and Martin Schongauer were painters.[4] Various documents and records have yielded comparatively little real information about any of Martin Schongauer's brothers.

Georg may have been the eldest; he has been assigned a birth-date of about 1445. After some initial training in his father's shop, it appears that he served his apprenticeship elsewhere, most likely in Strasbourg. He married Apollonia von Leyden, daughter of the great Strasbourg sculptor, Nicolaus Gerhaert von Leyden. Later he moved to Basel where the first document of his presence there is dated 1482. A decade later, still resident in Basel, Georg Schongauer was host to the young Albrecht Dürer when he arrived there from his visit to the surviving Schongauer brothers in Colmar in 1492. As nearly as can be determined, Georg Schongauer died between 1495 and 1514.

Paul Schongauer may have been Caspar's second son. He became a citizen of Leipzig in 1478. In 1489 his presence is documented in Basel. By 1492, however, he had returned to Colmar where he lived until his death in 1516.

---

[1] Most of the surviving documents pertaining to the life of Martin Schongauer and a number of the earliest published accounts of his life and career have been collected in the monograph by Julius Baum, *Martin Schongauer*, Vienna, 1948, Chapter VI, "Urkunden und sonstige Quellen zur Lebensgeschichte," pp. 66–70. Baum's monograph, and that by Eduard Flechsig, *Martin Schongauer*, Strasbourg, 1951, contain the most extensive recent accounts of Schongauer's life and the present interpretation of these documents.

[2] Baum, *Schongauer*, pp. 9–10; Flechsig, *Schongauer*, pp. 35–39. The family presumably originated in Schongau, a town thirty-eight miles south of Augsburg.

[3] Baum, *Schongauer*, documents 1 and 2, p. 66. I have used the word "citizen" to indicate the official, fully-endowed rights of a burgher. All residents of a town or city, whether born there or not, had to be enrolled on the *Bürgerrolle* in order to enjoy these full civic rights and freedoms.

[4] Flechsig, *Schongauer*, pp. 55–80, presents the fullest discussion.

Of "Caspar Schongauer III," who is also said to have been a goldsmith, there is no significant record except for the account of Dürer's visit to Colmar in 1492 written by Christoph Scheurl at Nuremberg in 1515.[5] According to Scheurl, Albrecht Dürer had been received kindly by the brothers Paul, Caspar, and Ludwig Schongauer. Their father had died before 1488, so it seems unlikely that Scheurl had confused the parent with his namesake son.[6]

Ludwig Schongauer became a painter. After early training, perhaps with Caspar Isenmann in Colmar, and probable apprenticeship at Ulm, he was enrolled as a citizen of Ulm in 1479. He later moved to Augsburg, the ancestral home of the Schongauer family, where he became a citizen in 1486. Later still, but at any rate by 1492, he returned to Colmar, and in 1493 he was made a citizen of Colmar. Soon thereafter, in January of 1494, he died. Hypothetically at least, Ludwig had returned to Colmar to take over the workshop of his brother Martin. He produced a few engravings of rather indifferent quality.[7]

There is not much more positive archival or documentary information concerning the details of Martin Schongauer's life than there is about the lives of his father and brothers. Indeed, considerable controversy has arisen over the interpretation of those records that do survive. Older interpretation has placed Martin Schongauer's birth-date as early as the 1420's, while recent scholars have suggested convincing reasons for placing it in the early 1450's. Although the balance of the evidence seems to point to the later date, proof on either side is still lacking.

"Martinus Schöngawer de Colmar" is listed on the matriculation register of the University of Leipzig in 1465. He is credited with payment of the standard fee of 10 groschen, and there seems no reason for doubting the identity of this enrollee. Those who support the earlier birth-date would explain Schongauer's matriculation at the university as a means to avoid the strictures of guild membership in Leipzig while executing a commission for the university. This may have been the case for another painter, Nikolaus Eisenberg, if it is he whose name (Nicolaus Ysenbergk) appears on the same matriculation list for 1465. Eisenberg, who was a Franciscan monk, was born about 1415. On the

matriculation list, Ysenbergk is credited for 6 groschen. This amount has been interpreted as a reduction of the fee in honor of his clerical status.[8] If, on the other hand, Martin Schongauer were entering the university as a regular student, an age of twelve to fifteen years would correspond to the practice of the time.

In any event, we may never know why Martin Schongauer travelled as far as Leipzig to enter the university. His brother Paul became a citizen of Leipzig thirteen years later, and it has been suggested that Paul Schongauer might have been a resident there as early as 1465, and have taken responsibility for his younger brother. Yet in the present interpretation of the documents, Paul himself would have only been in his later teens at the time, and thirteen years does seem a very long time for a journeyman apprenticeship at Leipzig without civic rights.

There is, further, a portrait of Martin Schongauer in the Alte Pinakothek in Munich, inscribed with his name and a date that ought to be more helpful than it is (fig. 1).[9] The inscription reads "Hipsch Martin Schongauer Maler." The date appears to be 1483. The escutcheon of the Schongauer family, a crescent gules on a field argent, appears with the inscription. The portrait itself is of an alert, youngish man with large features, apparently in his late twenties or early thirties.

On the back of the panel is a tattered, fifteenth-century scrap of paper on which is written:

Mayster Martin schongawer maler genent
    Hipsch
martin von wegen seiner kunst geborn zu
zu Kolmar Aber von Seinen öltern ain
augsburger bur(ger) des geschlechtze vo(n)
    her(ren)
geporn ze is (gesto)rben zu Kolm(ar) anno
    1499
(am) 2te (Tag) Hornungs dem got genad.

Ich sein junger hans burgkmair im jar 1488.

("Master Martin Schongauer, painter; called 'Hübsch Martin' [hübsch = 'handsome' or 'fair'] because of his art; born at Colmar but, through his parents, a burgher of Augsburg of a patrician family; died at Colmar in the year 1499 on the second

[5] Baum, *Schongauer,* document 21, pp. 70–71.

[6] Flechsig, *Schongauer,* pp. 57 and 70, indicates his strong doubt that the Caspar Schongauer mentioned by Scheurl (and nowhere else in the records or reminiscences of the Schongauers) was actually a brother of Martin Schongauer.

[7] A single example of each of four engravings by Ludwig Schongauer survives. They are described in Max Lehrs, *Geschichte und kritischer Katalog des deutschen, niederländischen und französischen Kupferstichs im XV. Jahrhundert,* VI, Vienna, 1927, pp. 61–63.

[8] Flechsig, *Schongauer,* pp. 87–108; Baum, *Schongauer,* pp. 12–14, and document 6, pp. 66–67. Flechsig presents a justifiable argument against identifying Nicolaus Ysenbergk as the painter. He points out that there is no reference to the person on the list as a cleric, as there is for certain others; that the name Eisenberg and its variants are common to the region; and that the reduction in fee could as easily represent a recognition of poverty or familial hardship on behalf of an entering student of the same name.

[9] Munich, Alte Pinakothek, Inv. No. 1027.

FIGURE 1   Thoman Burgkmair(?), retouched by Hans Burgkmair, *Portrait of Martin Schongauer*, panel, 1483, Alte Pinakothek, Munich.

day of February; by the grace of God. I, Hans Burgkmair, [was] his apprentice in the year 1488.")

The year 1499 has been entered by another hand than that of the main body of the text. The last line is by still another hand, that of Hans Burgkmair (1472–1515), who was, indeed, an apprentice in Martin Schongauer's shop, probably in 1488.[10] Martin Schongauer did not die in 1499, nor did he die in Colmar. His was not actually a patrician family; neither could he be considered a burgher of Augsburg. In all, the inscription pasted on the reverse of the Munich panel is of very limited value.

Schongauer's portrait is still listed by the Alte Pinakothek among the works by Hans Burgkmair (reworked by Burgkmair over an original apparently done by the Master of the Legend of St. Ulrich).[11] More convincing is Flechsig's contention that the portrait was painted by Thoman Burgkmair of Augsburg, the father of Hans Burgkmair.[12] At any rate, there has been considerable overpainting of the surface.

The Munich museum also interprets the date in the inscription on the front of the panel as 1453 rather than 1483. The confusion has arisen because the third digit of the date most closely resembles a capital "S." Flechsig, in his long discussion of the painting, has argued convincingly for the later date.[13] Baum has also concluded that the date is probably 1483, with the alternate proviso that if it is indeed 1453, then it represents Martin Schongauer's birth-date.[14]

On little more than this evidence, Schongauer's birth has been set at "1453(?)" by several modern scholars. Flechsig, who believed that Schongauer was born in 1452, has even suggested that the artist was born or christened on November 11 of that year because that is St. Martin's day.[15] It is more likely that the name "Martin" is simply further evidence for Martin Schongauer's birth in one of the houses on the Schedelgasse in Colmar, for the street is in the parish of St. Martin's church.

Additional evidence that Martin Schongauer was born in the early 1450's rather than the much earlier date once generally accepted, has been provided by Albrecht Dürer. On a drawing, now lost, was a note written in Dürer's own hand:

Dz hat der hubsch martin gerissen im 1470 jor

do er ein jung gsell was. Dz hab ich A.D. erfarn und im zu eren doher geschriben im 1517 jor.[16]

("This was drawn by hübsch Martin in the year 1470 when he was a young journeyman. I A[lbrecht] D[ürer] have acquired this and inscribed it to honor him in the year 1517.") Dürer, who certainly knew the details of Martin Schongauer's life, may be considered to have provided the most convincing and important evidence of all in the discussion of the question.

There is no further record of Martin Schongauer's presence at the University of Leipzig after the year 1465. The later matriculation records do not bear his name. By 1466 it is evident that he had returned to Colmar, there to begin his apprentice years learning the craft of painting. Though the history of his life during that period remains conjectural, his teacher was probably the aforementioned Caspar Isenmann, the leading painter of Colmar in that period, and a neighbor of the Schongauer family.

Until 1469, it appears, Martin Schongauer worked in Isenmann's shop, performing the tasks and acquiring the skills required by his chosen profession. In 1469 or 1470 he became a journeyman and probably undertook the travels traditionally expected of all young artisans at the conclusion of apprenticeship. The extent of the travels of the young Schongauer is unknown, but speculation has encouraged all writers to extend the journey to many German, French, and Netherlandish centers. A sojourn in Spain is also assumed by nearly all scholars, mostly on the basis of Hispano-Moorish features which include Negro facial types, costume details, and the flora and fauna of several early works. One of Schongauer's drawings, dated 1469, is a copy of the figure of Christ in Roger van der Weyden's *Last Judgment* Altarpiece in the Hôtel-Dieu in Beaune, so Schongauer probably visited that Burgundian city as well.[17] It is also likely that the strong Netherlandish influence on his paintings and prints reflects a direct knowledge of works in the Flemish centers.

The next important and fixed date in the life of Martin Schongauer appears on his painting of the *Madonna and Child in a Rose Arbor* (fig. 2). The painting was probably made for the church of St. Martin in Colmar, where it can still be seen. The

[10] See Tilman Falk, *Hans Burgkmair; Studien zu Leben und Werk des Augsburger Malers*, Munich, 1968, p. 9 and note 12, p. 87.
[11] *Altdeutsche Malerei; Katalog II, Alte Pinakothek*, Munich, 1963, no. 1027, pp. 50–52.
[12] Flechsig, *Schongauer*, pp. 1–33.
[13] Hans Burgkmair's *Self-Portrait as a Bridegroom*, a pen-and-wash drawing in the Albertina in Vienna, is inscribed with the date 1498. The last digit is written exactly like the "S" in the date of the portrait. See Falk, *Burgkmair*, fig. 10.

[14] Baum, *Schongauer*, p. 11.
[15] Flechsig, *Schongauer*, p. 33. Martin Luther, for example, was born on November 10, 1483, and baptized on November 11.
[16] Baum, *Schongauer*, p. 17 and document 11b, p. 67; Flechsig, *Schongauer*, pp. 30–32.
Munich, 1923, no. 23. The date and Martin Schongauer's mono-
[17] Jakob Rosenberg, *Martin Schongauer; die Handzeichnungen*, gram were added by Albrecht Dürer.

date, 1473, appears on the reverse of the panel. The present date, in fact, is a restoration of the original, but its authenticity is unquestioned. It establishes the early recognition of Martin Schongauer's accomplishment as a painter.

The name of Martin Schongauer is mentioned in the tax and rental records of the 1470's and '80's in the archives of the town of Colmar, though no record survives of his application or admittance to full citizenship rights (*Bürgerrechts*) there.[18] In the latter part of 1482, he may have been in Sölflingen, near Ulm, executing a commission for the cloister of the Clarissan Sisters there.[19] His brother Ludwig was then resident in Ulm. It would also seem logical for Martin Schongauer to have extended his journey from that region to Augsburg, his family's ancestral city. It must have been there that he met Thoman Burgkmair and possibly on the same journey that he sat, in 1483, for the initial portrait that survives in its retouched form in Munich's Alte Pinakothek.

In 1488, Martin Schongauer made both a personal and a family donation to the church of St. Martin in Colmar.[20] In the following year he changed his residence to Breisach, a Rhine River town between Colmar and Freiburg im Breisgau, where he became a citizen sometime before June 15, 1489. There he had obtained a huge and quite unusual commission from the church of St. Stephen, the Münster of Breisach. He was engaged to paint,

on the west, north, and south walls of the first nave bay, an immense depiction of the Last Judgment.

Death struck Martin Schongauer in Breisach on February 2, 1491 when he was probably about forty years old. It appears that his death occurred during an epidemic of the plague, ever a threat to port cities and towns.[21] He had not completed the fresco, nor had he brought to fulfillment the promise that all his works—products of his youth and early maturity—exhibited to his contemporaries. His efforts in painting, few as they are, show a lively awareness of the past in Alsatian, Rhenish, and Netherlandish art. They reflect a personal contribution to the evolution of these regionalisms into an integral German art.

His engravings have still further significance, for they represent a turning point in graphic art from an elegant, but minor and regional craft, to an international and major form of artistic expression. No graphic artist before Dürer contributed as much. Dürer, no more than twenty years Schongauer's junior, must have known this well when, in 1490, he set out at the end of his own apprenticeship with the certain intention of entering Martin Schongauer's shop. The direct influence of Schongauer's prints on the early woodcuts and engravings of Albrecht Dürer is only part of the proof of Martin Schongauer's impact on his contemporaries and on succeeding generations. But his central position in the evolution of artistic concepts in Germany is thus made very evident.

---

[18] Baum, *Schongauer*, documents 12 and 13, p. 68; Flechsig, *Schongauer*, pp. 122–38.

[19] Baum, *Schongauer*, p. 21 and document 14, pp. 68–69.

[20] Baum, *Schongauer*, document 15, p. 69.

[21] Baum, *Schongauer*, p. 24.

The Paintings

ACCORDING to the suppositions of most modern scholars, Martin Schongauer received his formal art training in the workshop of Caspar Isenmann, the leading painter in Colmar at that time. An old tradition which held that he studied in the shop of Roger van der Weyden has generally been abandoned in recent years.[1] The great Brussels painter had died in 1464, too early at any rate to have personally guided the young apprentice. On the other hand, Isenmann, who may himself have been trained in the Netherlands, was well able to impart more than simple technical training. The few surviving panel paintings and frescoes left to us from the hand of Martin Schongauer show an awareness of the major artistic trends of fifteenth-century northern Europe. Van der Weyden's influence, so clearly visible in Schongauer's works, is therefore inescapable.

Schongauer's awareness of the artistic trends of his time is crucial to his position in the development of copper-plate engraving. It sets him apart from most of his predecessors. Hypothetically at least, the art of engraving originated in the goldsmith's shop for the tools of the engraver are basically the same as those of the goldsmith. Martin Schongauer surely learned their use in his father's workshop. There is no evidence, on the other hand, that Caspar Isenmann ever practiced engraving or could offer his apprentice any technical training in that art. Thus it was a combination of experiences that formed Martin Schongauer's expression in graphic art.

His paintings, however, afford us the clearest insight into that aspect of his work that was most directly affected by Isenmann's training and influence. Unfortunately, there are too few works surviving, and these mostly too small in scale, too fragmentary, or too poorly preserved, to give us a balanced, comprehensive understanding of the artist as painter. Yet from them we do know his stylistic approach and we can understand something of the influences that affected his work. An awareness of these influences is as important for studying the prints as for understanding the paintings.

THE MADONNA AND CHILD IN A ROSE ARBOR

The only dated painting (1473) by Martin Schongauer is the *Madonna and Child in a Rose Arbor* in St. Martin's Church in Colmar (fig. 2).[2] It is surely the most famous of Schongauer's paintings. According to our present knowledge it is an early work, perhaps the earliest of all the surviving paintings. It is large in scale (2.00 x 1.15 meters), direct in its imagery, and possessed of a reserved and dignified sophistication. The Madonna, more than life-sized, is seated upon a banked-earth, grassy bench, above which rises a richly-flowering rose arbor. At least eight multicolored songbirds are perched in the branches of the rose-vines. The Virgin holds the nude Christ-child seated upon her left arm. Over her head, at the top center of the panel, hover two angels holding a large crown between them. An abbreviated inscription is still legible on Mary's gold halo: "Me carpes genito tu qu(oque) O S(an)ctissi(m)a V(irgo)" ("Pluck me also for thy son, O holiest Virgin"). All the features of the painting are silhouetted against a rich, formal, gold background.

A small and fairly early copy of the *Madonna in a Rose Arbor* is preserved today in the Isabella Stewart Gardner Museum in Boston (fig. 3).[3] Although many details of the original do not appear in the copy, it aids in reconstructing those areas of the original work that were lost when it was cut down on all four sides at some indeterminate date between the sixteenth and nineteenth centuries.[4] We

---

[1] See the communication of Lambert Lombard to Giorgio Vasari, dated April 27, 1565: "In Germania si levò poi un Bel Martino, tagliatore in rame, il quale non abandonò la maniera di Rogiero, suo maestro, ma non arrivò però alla bontà del suo colorire . . ." (Baum, *Schongauer,* document 9, p. 67; E. Buchner, *Martin Schongauer als Maler,* Berlin, 1941, pp. 50–78).

[2] Buchner, *Martin Schongauer als Maler,* pp. 79–101; Flechsig, *Schongauer,* pp. 340–54; Baum, *Schongauer,* pp. 49–51.

[3] P. Hendy, *The Isabella Stewart Gardner Museum, Catalogue*

of the Exhibited Paintings and Drawings, Boston, 1931; C. Kuhn, *A Catalogue of German Paintings in American Collections,* New York, 1936, no. 169.

[4] The irregular shape of the panel in its present condition is concealed by a too ornate modern frame. This irregularity of shape suggests that the painting was badly damaged at some time and that the damaged areas were removed and the shape of the panel then roughly balanced, rather than that the whole was cut down as a fashionable reworking.

FIGURE 2 Martin Schongauer, *Madonna and Child in a Rose Arbor,*
panel, 1473, St. Martin's Church, Colmar.

FIGURE 3 Anonymous German, *Madonna and Child in a Rose Arbor,* copy after
Schongauer, panel, ca. 1500(?), Isabella Stewart Gardner Museum, Boston.

may feel confident that Schongauer's painting originally depicted God the Father and the dove of the Holy Spirit in the heavens above the crown-bearing angels. The arbor and ground plants were more extensive, and the Virgin's robes were at no point cut off as they are in the surviving panel.

Only one scholar, Eduard Flechsig, has ever published a serious proposal that the Boston painting served as Schongauer's model, rather than the opposite.[5] In Flechsig's opinion, the Boston painting is a study for the altarpiece made by Schongauer himself. However, the small scale of the Boston panel, its loss of detail, and the hardening of features such as the folds of garments and the Virgin's hands are sure signs of a copyist. Other such signs are changes in the foliage of the rose arbor, which have turned the plants into bushes somewhat arbitrarily intertwined in the frame, rather than the carefully trained vines of the original. Also, in the Boston version, the face of the bench on which Mary sits is revealed as rather vacuous undefined space on either side of her garments. Schongauer's Virgin is enclosed within the lattice which extends forward on either side from the vertical posts. The copy shows the Virgin in a far less defined area and in a puzzling scale relationship to everything about her.

There is no particularly novel or unusual imagery in the iconography of Martin Schongauer's *Madonna in a Rose Arbor*. All of the individual flowers—roses, iris, lilies, strawberries, and columbine—visible or assumed in the original through the Boston copy, have been associated with Mary in studies of the flower symbolism of late Gothic painting.[6] The depiction of the Virgin seated on the earth is a standard representation of the "Virgin of Humility."[7]

Because of stylistic similarities, the Virgin, the Child, and the hovering angels with the crown in the *Madonna in a Rose Arbor* have often been compared to those in Schongauer's engraving of the *Madonna and Child on a Crescent*, (L.40).[8] The three-quarter length Madonna in the engraving appears above a crescent moon and a rumple of clouds; sun rays are radiating behind her and the angels hold a crown emblazoned with twelve stars. She is as emphatically the Apocalyptic Queen of Heaven as the one in the *Madonna in a Rose Arbor* is the

Queen of Earth. The contrast seems unquestionably deliberate.

Neither the *Madonna in a Rose Arbor* nor any other of the paintings attributed to Martin Schongauer is signed. All of the other attributions employ some combination of long-standing tradition and scholarly judgment based on comparison with the engravings or this large altarpiece. But the symmetry, the gold background, and the long tradition for representing the Virgin and Child in a rose arbor or garden, present some limitations for our judgment of the artist's style.

The figure-style, facial types, and draperies in the painting are, however, closely comparable to works by Roger van der Weyden such as the half-length *Madonna and Child* in the Gallery at Donaueschingen.[9] The pronounced influence of the Flemish master on the art of Martin Schongauer is, of course, no longer as surprising as it once seemed, since there are clear precedents for it in German art by the mid-fifteenth century. But the relationship is so close that it is easy to see why it was thought that Schongauer had studied in Roger's shop. Erwin Panofsky could properly say of Roger that "his very spirit was resurrected on German soil by Martin Schongauer."[10]

THE ORLIAC ALTARPIECE WINGS

Jean d'Orliac was preceptor of the Antonite monastery in Isenheim from 1466 until 1490. His portrait as donor appears on the inner right wing of a pair of painted altarpiece wings preserved in the Unterlinden Museum in Colmar (figs. 4, 5).[11] They are a part of an altarpiece once in a side-chapel of the monastery church. Like Grünewald's great altarpiece wings completed in 1515 for the high altar of the church, these wings appear to have opened upon a sculptured central image. In this case the sculpture was probably a statue of the Virgin now preserved in the Louvre.[12]

The outer sides of the two wings depict the Annunciation. On the inner left wing is an abbreviated Nativity scene. St. Anthony, patron of the monastery, appears on the inner right wing towering over the tiny donor-figure of Jean d'Orliac.

[5] Flechsig, *Schongauer,* pp. 341–45.

[6] See, for example, R. A. Koch, "Flower Symbolism in the Portinari Altarpiece," *Art Bulletin,* XLVI, 1964, pp. 70–77, with additional bibliography.

[7] For the iconography of the "Madonna of Humility" see M. Meiss, "The Madonna of Humility," *Art Bulletin,* XVIII, 1936, pp. 434ff; E. Panofsky, *Early Netherlandish Painting,* Cambridge, Mass., 1953, I, pp. 127ff.

[8] Baum, *Schongauer,* pp. 50–51.

[9] Panofsky, *Early Netherlandish Painting,* II, fig. 374.

[10] Panofsky, *Early Netherlandish Painting,* I, p. 308.

[11] Buchner, *Martin Schongauer als Maler,* pp. 56–78; Flechsig, *Schongauer,* pp. 383–87; Baum, *Schongauer,* pp. 51–52. Jean d'Orliac also appears as donor on the central, carved portion of the Isenheim Altarpiece. He kneels at the feet of St. Augustine facing the central image of St. Anthony. The statues were carved by Nicolas von Hagenau (Niklas Hagnower). It was Jean d'Orliac's successor, Guido Guersi, who commissioned Grünewald's famous wings of 1513–15.

[12] Illustrated, for example, by C. Sommer, "Madonnenfiguren am Oberrhein," *Oberrheinische Kunst,* I, 1925–26, p. 15.

FIGURE 4 Martin Schongauer, *Annunciation*, outer wings of the Orliac Altarpiece, panel, ca. 1470–80, Unterlinden Museum, Colmar.

Stylistically the wings of the Orliac Altarpiece are closely related to the *Madonna in a Rose Arbor,* sufficiently so, in fact, to conclude that they are the work of Martin Schongauer in the 1470's.[13] Here too, the figures are large in scale and appear in an extremely limited and formal spatial arrangement. The figure proportions and features, even the drapery style and gestures, are close to those of the altarpiece in St. Martin's church of Colmar and are similarly related to the style of Roger van der Weyden.

The iconographic content of the Orliac wings is also a simple continuation of well-precedented tradition. The angel's words at the Annunciation are carefully printed on a banderole entwined around the scepter that he carries. On the Virgin's halo appear the prophetic words of Isaiah: "Ecce virgo concipiet et pariet filiu(m) et vocabitu(r) nome(n) ei(us) Em(m)anuel" (Isa. 7:14). Above the angel is the figure of God the Father, his head and shoulders appearing through a cloud-framed opening in the sky. In his left hand, he holds a crystal orb surmounted by a cross. His gaze is directed downward toward the Virgin. The dove of the Holy Spirit appears on the Virgin's panel, descending from the direction of the figure of God. At the Virgin's feet is a pitcher containing a lily stalk with four blossoms and three buds. The seven flowers here, in company with the dove, may surely be interpreted as symbolic of the seven gifts of the Holy Spirit.[14] The lily, of course, is also the symbol of the Virgin's purity. It is present in various vessels in Annunciation pictures over several centuries. Behind the two figures the space is cut off by a sagging embroidered drapery. The angel's wings are patterned with the "eyes" characteristic of peacock feathers. Martin Schongauer made two engravings of the Annunciation, both probably of a later date than the Orliac wings (L.1 and L.2–3). Each retains comparative simplicity of design, but they both represent a considerable advance in sophistication and style.[15]

The inner left wing shows the Virgin adoring the new-born Christ-child. She kneels on the ground before a woven, wattle fence, arms crossed over her breast, gazing downward at the child who lies on a hem of her robe and gestures toward her in blessing. At the upper right corner of the panel is a figure of God the Father, gesturing in blessing downward toward the mother and child. With his left hand, he supports a globe surmounted by a cross. The ground is carpeted with wild strawberry plants.

The scene on this wing is usually called the *Nativity.* However, there are no other figures present, no localizing features, and the inscription, now barely visible on the halo of the Virgin, "Virgo quem genuit adorat," suggests that the image is more an isolated votive picture—a type of *Andachtsbild.*

The inner right wing portrays St. Anthony, the patron saint of the monastery at Isenheim. He carries a book of the scriptures and a Tau-headed staff in his left hand. Behind the saint, to the right, is a small pig, another of St. Anthony's attributes. The celebrated hermit saint gazes to the left, toward the missing central statue of the altarpiece. The background is a patterned gold field. In the lower left of the panel, also facing the central figure, kneels Jean d'Orliac, hands lifted in prayer. His coat-of-arms appears in the lower left corner.

THE HOLY FAMILY (Munich)

In the Alte Pinakothek in Munich there is a tiny (26 x 17 cm.) panel painting usually called the *Holy Family* (fig. 6).[16] Unsigned, it is attributed to Martin Schongauer by style and long tradition and generally accorded a relatively early place in his career. The painting depicts the Virgin, clad in beautiful red garments, holding the small, plump Christ-child on her lap and offering him a blue flower. The Virgin is seated upon a hummock of earth, and at her feet, along the bottom edge of the panel, are various plants and flowers. The two figures are isolated from the near middle ground except for a tiny path at the right. In the middle ground is the shed of the Nativity. The traditional ox and ass appear within the shed, and the small figure of St. Joseph is at the doorway, gazing contemplatively at the Mother and Child. Joseph is dressed in grey-blue with a bright red turban. Mary is magnificently silhouetted against the dark interior of the shed. The structure rises above the horizon so that the intricate rustic framework of its roof appears boldly against the bright blue and cream colors of the sky. A diminutive landscape is visible to the left. Distant blue mountains rise above the craggy, tree-topped cliffs of foothills. Sheep graze

---

[13] Flechsig, *Schongauer,* p. 386, on the contrary, argues for a date of 1488.

[14] From Isaiah 11:1–2. The seven gifts are: *sapientia, intellectus, consilium, fortitudo, scientia, pietas,* and *timor domini.* They are variously symbolized in other Annunciation pictures. For example, they appear as seven rays of light in Robert Campin's Mérode Altarpiece and in Jan van Eyck's *Annunciation in a Church,* both illustrated in Panofsky, *Early Netherlandish Painting,* II, figs. 204, 238.

[15] See pp. 33–34.

[16] Buchner, *Martin Schongauer als Maler,* pp. 102–06, 180–81; Flechsig, *Schongauer,* p. 393; Baum, *Schongauer,* p. 58.

FIGURE 5   Martin Schongauer, *Nativity; St. Anthony and the Donor, Jean d'Orliac,*
inner wings of the Orliac Altarpiece, panel, ca. 1470–80, Unterlinden Museum, Colmar.

FIGURE 6   Martin Schongauer, *Holy Family,* panel, ca. 1480, Alte Pinakothek, Munich.

in hillocked pasture land beyond a pond and marsh.

Intricate and detailed as all of this background scenery is, the figures of Mary and the Christ-child are distinct from the remainder of the composition, centered as a vertically extended pyramid rising two-thirds of the height of the panel. Even the raised foot of St. Joseph, painted in mid-stride, does not distract from the basic repose, formal harmony, and subtle balance of the central figures. This Mary, seated upon the ground, represents a "Madonna of Humility" very much like the Virgin in the *Madonna in a Rose Arbor.*

Even though the environment of the painting is that of the Nativity, the formal representation of the Virgin and Child is more closely comparable to the Colmar Madonna and to Schongauer's other versions of the Madonna such as the engraving of the *Madonna and Child on a Grassy Bench* (L.36) than to his versions of the Nativity per se. The additional features of the painting—St. Joseph, the ox and ass, the shed, and the grazing sheep—are more a part of the symbolic system. As attributes, they emphasize the theme of the Virgin's humility in accepting her role in the history of God become man.[17]

THE ADORATION OF THE
SHEPHERDS

The Berlin-Dahlem Museum possesses a small painting of the *Adoration of the Shepherds* (fig. 7).[18] It is generally accepted as a mature work by Martin Schongauer. The Christ-child is shown lying upon a white swaddling cloth on a saddle-blanket cushioned with straw against the rough stable floor. The Virgin is kneeling at the feet of the Child, her hands pressed together in prayerful adoration. Behind her, idly clasping his hands, stands St. Joseph. He is a larger, more imposing figure than the Joseph in the Munich painting. At the far right of the painting, near the head of the Christ-child, are three adoring shepherds, remarkably lifelike and vital figures. The heads of the ox and ass, in the shed behind the group of the Holy Family, are in line above the tiny body of the Christ-child. In the distance, beyond the rudely carpentered shed and the crumbling, overgrown walls of a tumbled stone building, is a deep landscape with rolling hills, rock outcroppings, sheep grazing in a meadow by a river,

and a distant town with a castle above it. The painting is tender and uncomplicated. It possesses a monumental quality not present in the Munich panel.

Compositionally, the *Adoration of the Shepherds* is comparable to the early engraving of the *Nativity* (L.5). The basic difference is the lack of enframement in the foreground plane. Only St. Joseph's gnarled walking stick with travel sacks knotted about it in the lower left corner, and a diagonal brace-beam in the upper right, set the limits of the space. The viewer is directly involved as a witness to the scene, with an intimacy and immediacy not characteristic of the early works. The mature engraving of the *Nativity* (L.4) shows the nature of Schongauer's change in approach.

In the *Adoration of the Shepherds* the perspective orthogonals in the structure of the shed generally converge near the head of St. Joseph, not to emphasize the saint, but to form a spatial organization that incorporates all of the figures. The long folds of the Virgin's garments also compare closely with those in later engravings, for example the series of "Wise and Foolish Virgins" (L.76–85). The massive figure of St. Joseph is reminiscent of the standing figures in the series of "Apostles" (L.41–52).

THE HOLY FAMILY (Vienna)

The tiny (26 x 17 cm.) panel of the *Holy Family* in the Kunsthistorisches Museum in Vienna also utilizes the setting of the Nativity (fig. 8).[19] Here the Christ-child stands in the lap of the Virgin, one foot and both arms raised in intent contemplation of a bunch of grapes that she holds. A book of the Scriptures is also on her lap. Behind the Mother and Child, through an arched opening on the left, appears St. Joseph, gazing at the pair and carrying a bundle of grain, presumably to feed the ox and ass whose heads are visible behind him. In the lower right foreground is a woven basket partially filled with grapes. St. Joseph's walking stick rests upon it. At the right, behind the Virgin, is an arched niche. A water canteen rests on its shelf. This work, too, is essentially a representation of the Virgin and Child with additional features that are to be interpreted more as attributes than environment. The space is arbitrary and undefined. The iconographic

[17] The concept is not Netherlandish. Rather it seems to go back to the International Gothic of the late fourteenth century. It was to be augmented in works by Dürer, Altdorfer, and others. Grünewald's *Virgin and Child with an Angel Concert*, the central panel of the second stage of the Isenheim Altarpiece, is an example of the redevelopment of this archaistic concept.

[18] Buchner, *Martin Schongauer als Maler*, pp. 106–10, 181; Flechsig, *Schongauer*, pp. 392–93; Baum, *Schongauer*, pp. 58–59.

[19] Buchner, *Martin Schongauer als Maler*, pp. 120–23, 181; Flechsig, *Schongauer*, p. 393; Baum, *Schongauer*, p. 59.

FIGURE 7 Martin Schongauer, *Adoration of the Shepherds,* panel, ca. 1480–90, Gemäldegalerie der Staatlichen Museen, Berlin.

FIGURE 8 Martin Schongauer, *Holy Family,* panel, ca. 1480–90, Kunsthistorisches
Museum, Vienna.

interpretation here, however, is considerably more subtle than that in the Munich or Berlin panels.

First of all, the grapes held by the Virgin represent a perennial symbol of Christ himself as the "True Vine." The bundle of grain carried by St. Joseph is primarily symbolic of the locale of the scene—Bethlehem signifies "House of Bread." The bundle of grain in the foreground of Hugo van der Goes's Portinari Altarpiece carries the same meaning. The stable of the Nativity was described as a virtual granary in the medieval *Legend of the Three Kings*.[20] By combining the grapes and grain, Schongauer sought to emphasize the eucharistic element in his localization of the event. The water canteen in the niche is a Marian symbol—a descendent of the water flask in a niche at the right of the Virgin in Jan van Eyck's *Lucca Madonna* in Frankfurt.[21] There, as here, its significance is derived from epithets for the Virgin—the "Fountain of Gardens" or "Well of Living Waters" or, perhaps better in this instance, the "Sealed Fountain" of the Song of Solomon (4:12).[22]

St. Joseph is more than an onlooker, then, in the Vienna *Holy Family*. It was he who gathered the grapes and provided the grain and the water canteen. He carries the latter slung over his back in the engraving of the *Flight into Egypt* (L.7). More than any other of Martin Schongauer's works, the Vienna panel reflects the growing stress on the importance of St. Joseph that is found in increasing numbers of fifteenth-century representations of Christ's foster-father.

The *Holy Family* in Vienna is generally accepted as a mature work, probably from the 1480's. The scale of the figures to the space and the severe limitations of the space itself seem characteristic of the developed works by Martin Schongauer. The space in the painting, in fact, is rather ambiguous; no landscape is visible and it appears that the Madonna is seated within the interior of the stable rather than in front of it. The light is diffused, without more than a general indication that it comes from the left.

THE MADONNA AND CHILD IN A CHAMBER

The Kuntsmuseum in Basel possesses a small (28 x 22 cm.) panel painting of the *Madonna and Child in a Chamber* (fig. 9).[23] It is usually accepted as an early work by Martin Schongauer. Unfortunately the face of the Virgin has been entirely repainted. However, the interior setting for the figures is delicately painted and quite beautiful. It derives clearly from elements in works by all three of the major early Netherlandish painters, Robert Campin, Roger van der Weyden, and Jan van Eyck. None of Martin Schongauer's other works displays such interest in interior environment, furnishings, or play of light as this small panel in Basel.

There are many curious features about the figures of the Virgin and Child. Mary's position is undeterminable. She is either seated or kneeling at a small prie-dieu, turning the pages of a small book that rests on a cushion atop the prie-dieu. With her left hand she supports the tiny infant who reclines in her lap with his right arm raised, but doubled back in an inexplicable gesture. The figure of the Virgin is huge in scale with the features of the room, which suggest a deliberate Campinesque archaism. Her unbelted tunic, flowing uninterrupted from neck and shoulders to a massive and undefined skirt, is also unusual for Martin Schongauer. She wears a heavy, tapestry-like undergarment with a jeweled hem. Similar garments appear in Campin's and Roger van der Weyden's paintings of the Virgin on occasion, though not with the disproportionate massiveness shown here.

Almost all of the features of the painting show an indebtedness to the Netherlands. That is the reason the work is considered to have been painted early in Schongauer's career, shortly after his return from the travels of his journeyman days. But the painting shows a different impact from Flemish painting than appears in the other works. Thus the attribution seems doubtful, despite the high quality of the painting. The work should not, perhaps, be entirely dismissed, but it is difficult to give it any secure place in Schongauer's stylistic development as a painter.

HIGH ALTAR OF THE DOMINICAN CHURCH (Colmar)

Sixteen panels, half of them painted with scenes on both sides, are the preserved remains of an altarpiece once on the high altar of the Dominican church in Colmar.[24] The altarpiece was replaced in 1749 and the panels are now in the Unterlinden Museum. Several of them are in poor condition,

[20] Johannes Hildesheimensis, *Liber trium regem*, ca. 1370, early English translation, ed. C. Horstmann, *The Three Kings of Cologne*, Early English Text Society, London, 1886, vol. 85.
[21] Panofsky, *Early Netherlandish Painting*, II, fig. 252.
[22] Panofsky, *Early Netherlandish Painting*, I, pp. 137, 143–44.

[23] Buchner, *Martin Schongauer als Maler*, pp. 51–53, 177; Flechsig, *Schongauer*, pp. 394–97; Baum, *Schongauer*, p. 57.
[24] Buchner, *Martin Schongauer als Maler*, pp. 166, 185–86 (as "School-work"); Flechsig, *Schongauer*, pp. 354–83; Baum, *Schongauer*, pp. 52–57.

FIGURE 9   Attributed to Martin Schongauer, *Madonna and Child in a Chamber,* panel,
ca. 1470–80, Oeffentliche Kunstsammlung, Basel.

and there is considerable repainting of the scenes. The work is traditionally assigned to Martin Schongauer's workshop and some of the panels have been attributed to his own hand. The best reconstruction is probably that in Baum's monograph.[25]

There are clear reflections of Martin Schongauer's works in the panels of this altarpiece. The strongest comparisons are with the engraved works. None of them, however, have the spatial, proportional, or design qualities of works from Martin Schongauer's hand. They have a pronounced provincial charm, particularly in paintings such as the *Christ Appearing to Mary Magdalene*.[26] The painting is clearly related to the engraving of the same subject (L.15), but comparison only emphasizes the differences in concept. More telling is the distinct relationship borne by various panels of the altarpiece to engravings from the entire chronological sequence of Schongauer's works. As far as the altarpiece of the Dominican Church is concerned, it must be concluded that the panels do not seem to have emerged from Schongauer's shop, or at least they were not done under his supervision.

THE NATIVITY (Frankfurt)

The Städelsches Kunstinstitut in Frankfurt possesses a small panel painting of the Nativity that is clearly related to Martin Schongauer's art (fig. 10).[27] The painting must either be a copy of a lost work by the artist or an original composition by a member of Schongauer's school. The setting is a tumbling, open-walled shed with a crisp, snowy, winter landscape beyond. In the center the Virgin kneels in adoration of the Child who lies before her in a stone manger. Three shepherds gaze in from the left. In the background, struggling up a path to the shed, is St. Joseph leading two women. These are the midwives sought out by the saint according to the account of the Nativity in the apocryphal gospel of Pseudo-Matthew.[28] The painter seems to have been familiar with the Munich, Berlin, and Vienna panels. In the Frankfurt *Nativity*, however, the contrasts of light and shadow effect a starkness of atmosphere and a rather vacuous quality of unfilled space. A rake lies across the foreground in place of Joseph's walking stick in the Berlin and Vienna panels. Here, instead of creating a space-defining foil for the painting, as Schongauer could

do with foreground objects, the careful centering of the rake serves only to trip the viewer's eye.

Additional differences between this painting and the work of Martin Schongauer can be seen by comparing it with the engraving of the *Nativity* (L.4). The painter seems to have been most strongly influenced by this engraving from Schongauer's mature period. But the subtle, geometric order of the composition in the engraving is lost. The fussy complexity of drapery goes far beyond Schongauer's own characteristic exuberance. These observations, however, cannot detract from the splendid naturalism of the sun-glare on snow, deep contrasting shadow, and the general charm of the painting.

MADONNA AND CHILD
AT A WINDOW

Several panel paintings of this theme survive in various collections, the best of which are the *Madonna and Child at a Window Crowned by Two Angels*, formerly in a private collection in Frankfurt, and the *Madonna and Child at a Window Crowned by an Angel*, in a private collection in Vienna.[29] The first of these is closely related to the engraving of the *Madonna and Child on a Crescent* (L.40); the second, to the *Madonna and Child with a Parrot* (L.37). Both paintings are devotional images showing the Virgin in half-length standing at a vertical, architectural aperture. Both display a conscious reiteration of themes in works by Roger van der Weyden. Baum suggests that the Frankfurt version is a very early work, the Vienna panel one of Martin Schongauer's most mature paintings.

THE LAST JUDGMENT

Certainly the most unusual of all Martin Schongauer's accomplishments was the immense composition of the *Last Judgment* that he painted on the west, north, and south walls in the western bay of the nave in the Münster at Breisach between 1489 and his death in 1491.[30] The advent of Gothic architecture in northern Europe three centuries earlier had effectively put an end to the huge projects of fresco decoration on church walls, thereby diverting the best artistic effort to stained-glass and sculptural pro-

[25] Baum, *Schongauer*, p. 54.
[26] Reproduced in color in Baum, *Schongauer*, pl. II facing p. 34.
[27] Buchner, *Martin Schongauer als Maler*, pp. 110–12, 182–83; Baum, *Schongauer*, p. 60.
[28] In his engraving of the *Nativity* (L.4), Schongauer shows

Joseph with only one midwife, following the account in chapter 14 of the *Protevangelion*.
[29] Buchner, *Martin Schongauer als Maler*, pp. 74–78, 115–19, 178, 181; Flechsig, *Schongauer*, pp. 392–93.
[30] Buchner, *Martin Schongauer als Maler*, pp. 128–55, 182; Flechsig, *Schongauer*, pp. 387–90; Baum, *Schongauer*, pp. 62–63.

FIGURE 10   Follower of Martin Schongauer, *Nativity,* panel, ca. 1490–1500, Städelsches
Kunstinstitut, Frankfurt.

grams. The Last Judgment became an element familiar on the portals of churches. Nevertheless, the tradition to which the Breisach church belongs can be traced to Carolingian and Ottonian churches no great distance from Breisach itself. Furthermore, a surprising number of Rhenish churches, from the fourteenth century onward, include reappearing versions of the Last Judgment in fresco on their vaults and west walls.[31]

Schongauer's version is not very well preserved. Most of the details, however, can still be seen. The composition, spread over three walls, follows well-established tradition, probably influenced by his memory of Roger van der Weyden's altarpiece in Beaune. The west wall shows the Judgment itself, with Christ seated on a rainbow surrounded by the Virgin, John the Baptist, apostles, prophets, and above, angels with the instruments of the Passion. Flanking the entry are the dead emerging from the earth. On the north wall is the flaming holocaust of Hell, filled with semi-human demons tormenting naked, pain-wracked souls. Angels guide the saved souls on the south wall upward to a gateway, while above, they are serenaded by an angel chorus on an elaborately balustraded balcony.

The *Last Judgment* proved to be Martin Schongauer's last work. He died in 1491, probably while he was still engaged in the completion of the fresco. He did not leave a particularly large or varied legacy of paintings by which to evaluate his contribution in this medium. Moreover, his paintings seem at first quite conservative, rather simple reiterations of themes already well established by preceding generations of fifteenth-century northern painters. It would be a mistake, however, to conclude that Schongauer's art represents nothing but provincial archaism. On the contrary, his paintings are deliberate in their simplicity and directness. Fully cognizant of the complex iconographical systems and schemes that characterize the great Netherlandish painters of the second and third quarters of the fifteenth century, Martin Schongauer set a different course. By the end of the century such archaism had extended to a "genuine revival" in the Netherlands itself.[32]

[31] P. Clemen, *Die gotischen Monumentalmalereien der Rheinlande,* Düsseldorf, 1930. Clemen discusses twenty-four examples from the thirteenth to the fifteenth century.

[32] Panofsky, *Early Netherlandish Painting,* I, pp. 307ff.

The Engravings

BETWEEN the early 1470's and his death in 1491, Martin Schongauer made one hundred and sixteen engravings. His fame has rested far more upon his creations in that medium than upon his paintings. Something in the studied intricacy of preparation that precedes the production of a finished engraving seems to have particularly suited Martin Schongauer's nature. The reduction of solid form and color to patterns of black line on a white surface inspired him to invest the engravings with more volumetric solids and more convincing space than are found in the colors and planes of his paintings.

Scholars are in agreement that all of the engravings by Martin Schongauer are known today. Each of his prints exists in plentiful numbers and all are signed with Schongauer's familiar monogram. None of them, on the other hand, bears a date. Therefore the basic evidence for dating the engravings is stylistic. A fairly convincing pattern for the chronology of the prints has emerged from the analytical observations of several scholars.[1]

It is safe to assume that almost every engraver until Albrecht Dürer's day, including Dürer himself, was trained, at least in part, in the shop of a goldsmith. Many engravers were practicing goldsmiths. It seems certain that the goldsmith Caspar Schongauer took part in the earliest training of his son, teaching him the use of tools that were instrumental in the evolution of printmaking. Martin Schongauer's subsequent training in the shop of the painter Caspar Isenmann enabled him to combine skills learned in the traditional and conservative milieu of the craftsman's shop with the wider viewpoint and creative stimulation of the painter's atelier. Only a few of Schongauer's engravings can be connected in any way with goldsmithery or seem to have been intentionally designed as patterns for work in any other medium.

Three fourths of Martin Schongauer's engravings depict religious subjects. Since none are taken from the Old Testament, the Biblical chronology begins with the Annunciation. The Lehrs *Katalog* of Schongauer's engravings groups the prints in divisions by category of subject in more or less traditional fashion. The following discussion of the prints follows Lehrs' numbering which varies in some particulars from that of Bartsch.[2]

THE ANNUNCIATION

Martin Schongauer produced two versions of the *Annunciation* in engraving. The first (L.1) was made in the early 1480's; the second (L.2 and 3), on two separate plates showing the Virgin and the archangel Gabriel, was made close to the end of his comparatively short career. Copies of the earlier *Annunciation,* dated 1484 and 1485 (Lehrs, *Katalog,* p. 40), aid in establishing the date. The setting in this print is quite ambiguous. It seems to be an open, low-walled terrace. The Virgin kneels on a wrinkled carpet in the right foreground. In front of her is a three-legged stool topped by a cushion. She holds an open book and glances back over her shoulder toward Gabriel. The archangel also kneels, with spread wings, behind Mary. He raises his right hand in blessing. In his left hand he holds a scepter and a corner of the drapery of a partially-open canopy. A banderole drifts, loosely entwined, around Gabriel's left hand and the scepter. God the Father appears in a radiance over the head of Gabriel. Long beams of light extend from the radiance downward toward the Virgin. Along them, between Gabriel and the figure of Mary, is the descending dove of the Holy Spirit. A low wall runs across the background behind the archangel and the canopy.

It is not easy to decipher the significance of the setting for this representation of the Annunciation. Nevertheless, the pattern of geometrical form, and of light contrasted with shadow, augments the en-

---

[1] Evidence for dating the prints by their influence on dated or datable works has produced no startling contradictions; see the list of such works in Baum, *Schongauer,* pp. 34–35. Baum's discussion of the prints in chronological order, pp. 31–44, is quite clear and is accepted by most modern scholars. Flechsig, *Schongauer,* pp. 317–21, lists the prints after his own interpretation of their sequence, which is according to the direction of light source and shadows. His long discussion, pp. 188–253, 282–317, incorporates some excellent observations. The general groupings seem fairly consistent, but the finer distinctions are over-particularized.

[2] Adam von Bartsch, *Le peintre graveur,* 21 vols., Vienna 1803–21. The abbreviation "B." is used to refer to this work.

counter of the two major figures beautifully. The antecedents of the figural composition are not obscure. The engraving shows a clear awareness of Netherlandish compositional treatment of the subject, visible in at least three paintings by or associated with Roger van der Weyden: the *Annunciation* in the Louvre, Paris, the left wing of the Columba Altarpiece in Munich, and the *Annunciation* in the Metropolitan Museum of Art in New York (fig. 11).[3] The engravings of the same subject by the Master E.S. (L.8–12) show the same Flemish influence as interpreted by that artist.

Though the basic figure composition can be traced much further back, to French and Franco-Flemish manuscript illumination, almost all of its interpreters chose an interior setting for the event. The unusual treatment by Martin Schongauer seems to indicate some further significance. First, the angel drawing back the hanging drapery of the canopy performs an act that in other artists' works is usually a gesture of revelation. In addition, the canopy itself is not a *Betthimmel* as Lehrs described it, but conforms to representations of throne canopies, as in the *Trinity* by Robert Campin in the Hermitage, Leningrad; the drawing of a *Sacra Conversazione* by the same artist in the Louvre, Paris; or the *Madonna and Saints* by Roger van der Weyden in the Städelsches Kunstinstitut in Frankfurt.[4] The Master E.S. used the form in his *Judgment of Solomon* (L.7) and in the *Madonna Enthroned with Eight Angels* (L.76). Gabriel's revelation to the Virgin in Schongauer's *Annunciation* engraving, then, is a revelation of her own regal role given to the "Mary of Humility." The canopy and stool seem to be meant as visual symbols of the Virgin's transformation effected by Gabriel's message.

The other representation of the *Annunciation* by Martin Schongauer is usually considered among his last works. The archangel and the Virgin are depicted on two separate sheets of equal size and format. No setting at all appears on either sheet, save a vague horizontal line that crosses each print behind the figures at ankle height. Both figures are large in spatial scale, nearly filling each plate. The voluminous robes worn by each fall in spendid rhythm. Gabriel holds a scepter entwined by a blank banderole. A hinged-lidded canister holds two budding and flowering lily stalks in the left foreground of the Virgin's half of the scene. With one of her long, tapered fingers she marks the place where she has been reading in a small book. The figures

are delineated in sculptural form created by carefully balanced light and shade distribution.

THE "LIFE OF THE VIRGIN" SERIES

There are also two engraved versions of the Nativity by Martin Schongauer. The earlier one (L.5) is the first of a set of four engravings, all among his earliest works, that depict the *Nativity, Adoration of the Magi, Flight into Egypt,* and *Death of the Virgin* (L.5, 6, 7, 16). This group, all of the same dimensions, is usually considered to be an incomplete series of scenes of the "Life of the Virgin." This conclusion has been influenced by the fact that Albrecht Dürer used some of the imagery in these engravings for his own large woodcut series of the "Life of the Virgin." But if we forget the disparate chronology of the four scenes, there does remain a conceptual balance in their meaning. We may wish for more, but the series is not merely a fragment.

Two of the engravings, the *Nativity* and the *Adoration of the Magi*, belong to the traditional Joys of the Virgin. The others, *Flight into Egypt* and *Death of the Virgin*, are numbered among her Sorrows. The *Nativity* shows the humble, private joy of Mary, attended only by St. Joseph, the two animals, and a small group of simple shepherds. The *Adoration of the Magi* represents the world's rejoicing at the event.[*] The kings, with pomp and splendor, offer obeisance and gifts of the world's wealth to their ruler. In the *Flight into Egypt*, the small miracle of the date tree, with its assurance of divine sustenance, does not overwhelm the arduousness of the journey or the implied tyrannical wrath of Herod that resulted in the Massacre of the Innocents. There is a private, humble sorrow here, shared only by St. Joseph, the burdened beast, and five diminutive angels. The *Death of the Virgin* implies the world's sharing in the sorrow of the event, for it is witnessed by the twelve apostles, summoned from all corners of the world at her deathbed by another miracle. But beyond the sorrow of the moment is the triumph of the Virgin's assumption, and the spread of the universal faith through the mission of the apostles.

The engraving of the *Nativity* in this series is more elaborate than any of Schongauer's panel

---

[3] See Panofsky, *Early Netherlandish Painting,* II, figs. 308, 309, for the *Annunciation* in the Louvre; figs. 352, 354, for the left wing of the Columba Altarpiece.

[4] Panofsky, *Early Netherlandish Painting,* II, figs. 210, 231, 332.

[*] An earlier impression, probably a trial proof, is preserved in New York, in the Metropolitan Museum's graphic collection, acc. no. 32.78.1. See W. M. Ivins, "An Undescribed Schongauer Trial Proof," *Metropolitan Museum Studies,* IV (1933), pp. 178f.

FIGURE 11   Attributed to Roger van der Weyden, *Annunciation*, panel, ca. 1450–60,
The Metropolitan Museum of Art, New York; gift of J. Pierpont Morgan, 1917.

paintings related to the subject. The Holy Family is gathered within one bay of a crumbling Gothic ruin. The architecture creates an impressive space, but the perspective is not constructed mathematically. Schongauer has mastered the visual perspective approach used by Jan van Eyck and Roger van der Weyden. The engraving is often compared to the central panel of Roger's Bladelin Altarpiece in Berlin. No doubt the altarpiece did influence Schongauer, but the reorientation of the architecture—so that the scene is viewed through the frame of a destroyed wall in the foreground—makes the scene more intimate and, simultaneously, more monumental.

Schongauer's *Nativity* was, in turn, a very influential work. Lehrs lists myriad copies in painting and sculpture in addition to eight direct copies in graphic media. An interesting example is the small panel attributed to Jan Jost (Joost) of Calcar in the Johnson Collection in Philadelphia (fig. 12); here the artist has transformed the scene into a night-time Nativity, perhaps influenced by the *Nativity* by Geertgen tot Sint Jans in the National Gallery, London.[5] Echoes of Schongauer's *Nativity* are also to be found in works by Dürer, Altdorfer, Holbein, and others.

The heavy lines, strong contrasts, and slightly sketchy quality of the drawing correspond to those engravings usually assigned to Martin Schongauer's earlier period. All four of the "Life of the Virgin" engravings are similar in this stylistic respect. Each is signed with a vertically-stemmed "M" in his monogram. This form of the monogram is present in a group of eleven engravings by the artist that are otherwise stylistically similar.[6] These are surely the first engravings in the chronology of Martin Schongauer's works.

The *Adoration of the Magi* (L.6) is a large print, in the same scale as the *Nativity*. The foreground setting is a Gothic architectural ruin, closely related to that depicted in the *Nativity*. The Virgin is seated on a wooden bench at the left holding the infant Christ in her lap. The eldest of the kings, his crown at the Virgin's feet, kneels before the Mother and Child. Mary has taken his offering of a gold vessel. The other two kings stand behind the first. The younger of these, on the right, is a negro, in accordance with the tradition that each of the Magi represented a separate continent. Europe,

Africa, and Asia were frequently indicated by the physiological types and the costumes of the three kings in fifteenth-century representations of the Adoration of the Magi.

The Magi are accompanied by an elaborate retinue. Banners fly, servants unpack saddle-bags, and a dog romps in the lower right corner. Above the thatched roof of the improvised stable blazes the star of Bethlehem. Iconographically, the representation of the Adoration of the Magi has changed little in Martin Schongauer's version from the Franco-Flemish portrayals of the subject painted at the outset of the fifteenth century.

The *Flight into Egypt* (L.7) belongs to the same series. The Holy Family has paused briefly at the edge of a grove of trees. St. Joseph has laid aside his walking stick and is gathering dates from a palm tree. His efforts are assisted by five tiny angels who have bent the tree to enable the old man to reach its fruit. Through the trees appear a buck deer and a doe. At the left edge of the scene is a towering tropical dragon tree (*Dracaena draco*). Three lizards scramble about the lower trunk and near its base. At the top left a parrot eats the berries in the uppermost branches.

The inclusion of such tropical exotica as the dragon tree has formed part of the argument of those scholars who believe that Martin Schongauer's youthful travels took him as far as Spain. The miracle of the bending palm tree is pictured in many fifteenth-century representations of the Flight of the Holy Family into Egypt. The account of it is recorded in the apocryphal gospel of the Pseudo-Matthew.[7] Schongauer's engraving was much copied. It also had a clear influence on the woodcut of the *Flight into Egypt* (B.89) in Albrecht Dürer's series of the "Life of the Virgin."

The Virgin and Child are central figures in the composition. The bent date palm arches gracefully over their figures. Mary sits on the back of the donkey, loosely holding a rein as the animal bends toward a thistle growing by the path. In her other hand she holds a date, managing at the same time to steady the infant on her lap. The engraving, like the others in the series to which it belongs, is an early work. The wealth of detail and the rather heavy and not entirely descriptive lines are characteristic. The most awkward section is at the ground behind the rear feet of the donkey where the heavy

[5] Panofsky, *Early Netherlandish Painting*, II, fig. 448.

[6] In addition to the "Life of the Virgin" series, these include: the *Man of Sorrows with the Virgin and St. John* (L.34); the *Madonna and Child with a Parrot* (L.37); the *Madonna and Child on a Crescent* (L.40); the *Tribulations of St. Anthony* (L.54);

[] *St. George and the Dragon* (L.58); the *Peasant Family Going to Market* (L. 90); and the *Bishop's Crozier* (L.106).

[7] A familiar example, painted about a decade after Schongauer's engraving, is the miniature by Jean Colombe in the *Très Riches Heures du duc du Berry*. See the illustration in Jean Longnon and Raymond Cazelles, *The Très Riches Heures of Jean, Duke of Berry*, New York, 1969, no. 57 (fol. 57r).

FIGURE 12   Attributed to Jan Joost, *Nativity,* panel, ca. 1500, Courtesy of the John G. Johnson Collection, Philadelphia.

shadow and direction of the lines seem to negate the space.

There are two states, with only slight changes in the second, of the engraving of the *Death of the Virgin* (L.16). Like the others in the series, it is an ambitious, extremely detailed portrayal of the event. The setting is a chamber within which the deathbed of the Virgin occupies most of the space. About it are gathered the twelve apostles. They perform the last rites for Mary who, still youthful in appearance, lies on the bed and is propped up by large cushions. A burning candle stands in an elaborate candlestick in the right foreground at the foot of the bed. Another is pressed into Mary's right hand. Schongauer has achieved an atmospheric expression of calm sorrow rather than agitated grief through the gestures and expressions of the participants.

That calm sorrow is the principal difference between Schongauer's *Death of the Virgin* and the similarly composed version of the subject by Hugo van der Goes (fig. 13). Hugo's painting, in the Groeninge Museum in Bruges, is probably a late work by the great Ghent artist, and may be the first instance of retroactive influence upon Flemish painting from the celebrated German emulator of Netherlandish art.[8] It is by no means a direct copy of Schongauer's engraving, since it includes an apparition of Christ and angels at the upper left. But there are similarities of composition, gestures, and distribution of figures that suggest a definite connection.

THE "LIFE OF CHRIST" SERIES

The second version of the *Nativity* (L.4) also appears to have been part of a series. During Schongauer's mature period he produced five prints that are all nearly square and of almost identical measurements. They include this *Nativity;* the *Baptism of Christ* (L.8); *Christ Appearing to Mary Magdalene* (L.15); *Christ Blessing the Virgin* (L.18); and *Christ Crowning the Virgin* (L.17). It has been suggested that the first three of these prints are part of an unfinished series of the "Life of Christ," but it seems more likely that the scenes are all related to each other as part of a series that is not simply narrative in content.[9]

The *Nativity* in this group is less elaborate than the early example. The Virgin is centered vertically in the square format. She kneels in adoration of the infant Christ, who lies on a corner of her robe atop a mound of hay in the lower right corner of the composition. There is far less emphasis on space. Instead, Schongauer has concentrated on the geometry of the scene, on the balance of light and shade, and on surface textures. The shed has been reduced to a minimal structure. Far in the background, at the left, St. Joseph brings a midwife to the stable, following the account of the Nativity in the apocryphal text of the *Protevangelion.* Three tiny caroling angels float together in the sky, and on a distant hillside a shepherd gazes upward from the midst of his flock. All of these, however, are reduced to incidental details, augmenting the silent communication between the Virgin and the Child.

The *Baptism of Christ* (L.8) is close in proportion and style to this second version of the *Nativity* (L.4). It, too, is a carefully-studied and balanced composition. There is little iconographic variation in representations of the Baptism of Christ from Roger van der Weyden's *St. John* Altarpiece, to the two engravings (L.28 and L.29) and the Louvre drawing by the Master E.S., and the present version by Schongauer.[10] St. John the Baptist is at the right on a rocky shelf over the Jordan River. He gestures, more or less in blessing, over the head of a youthful Christ who stands in the stream facing him. At the right is an angel holding Christ's robe, and in the sky appear God the Father and the dove of the Holy Spirit. In the background the river widens to a vast bay, bordered by bleak rocks and distant mountains. The engraving belongs among the mature works by Martin Schongauer as the sure drawing and delicate modeling attest. The formal balance of the composition, the echoes of diagonals and verticals in gestures and folds, and the general proportions are quite in keeping with the style of the later engraving of the *Nativity* (L.4).

The engraving of *Christ Appearing to Mary Magdalene* (L.15) maintains the careful balance and design rhythm established in the *Nativity* and the *Baptism.* Mary Magdalene kneels at the left on a low shelf of earth that sweeps in from the left. On its lip rests the ointment jar. The Magdalene reaches her right hand toward Christ, who stands at the left bearing the standard of his victory over

[8] Alan Shestack, *Fifteenth Century Engravings of Northern Europe from the National Gallery of Art*, Washington, D.C., 1967, no. 41; but for a contrary view see Panofsky, *Early Netherlandish Painting*, I, note 337/5, pp. 501f.

[9] Alan Shestack, *Fifteenth Century Engravings*, no. 76, has suggested that the three narrative scenes belong together. Baum,

Schongauer, p. 41, lists all five as part of an uncompleted series.

[10] Roger van der Weyden's *St. John* Altarpiece in Berlin is illustrated, for example, by Panofsky, *Early Netherlandish Painting*, II, figs. 342, 344. The Louvre drawing of the *Baptism of Christ* by the Master E.S. and his engraving of the same subject (L.29) appear in Alan Shestack, *The Master E.S., Five Hundredth Anniversary Exhibition*, Philadelphia, 1967, nos. 83, 84.

FIGURE 13 Hugo van der Goes, *Death of the Virgin,* panel, ca. 1481, Bruges, Groeninge Museum.

death, a cross-staff with a pennant emblazoned with the cross. Christ, displaying the wounds of the Crucifixion, gestures in restraint toward the Magdalene, his gesture implying the words "Touch me not; for I am not yet ascended to my Father . . ." (John 20:17). The composition is traditional and bears the unmistakable influence of *Christ Appearing to Mary Magdalene* (L.48) by the Master E.S. Schongauer has dropped the older tradition that depicts Christ carrying a gardener's shovel (used by his predecessor), illustrating the Magdalene's confusion of the resurrected Christ with a gardener as related in the Gospel of St. John (20:15).

The engravings of *Christ Crowning the Virgin* (L.17) and *Christ Blessing the Virgin* (L.18) are also very similar in proportion, style, and compositional arrangement to the narrative scenes of the *Nativity* (L.4), *Baptism* (L.8), and *Christ Appearing to Mary Magdalene* (L.15), with which, as already noted, they form part of a series.

Most of the representations of the Virgin's coronation in fifteenth-century engravings follow the tradition of showing the three persons of the Trinity present. Schongauer has chosen the older tradition of thirteenth- and fourteenth-century art in representing Christ alone crowning Mary.[11] The engraving of *Christ Blessing the Virgin* may derive from the version by the Master E.S. (L.36), as Shestack has observed.[12] The same scene appears as a substitute for the Coronation of the Virgin in the beautiful *Hours of Catherine of Cleves* in the Morgan Library in New York (fig. 14).[13] Both of Schongauer's engravings are mature works, balanced in design, simple in setting, and fine-lined in execution. The sweet, regular features of the faces are typical of this phase of Schongauer's career. Their rather vacuous expressions contrast quite sharply with the expressive features in early works such as the engraving of *Christ Carrying the Cross* or the series of the "Passion of Christ."

CHRIST CARRYING THE CROSS
AND THE CRUCIFIXION
OF CHRIST

The large engraving of *Christ Carrying the Cross* (L.9) is probably the most famous of all Martin Schongauer's engravings. The huge print shows over fifty figures in a sweeping processing from right to left, arrested at the center by the two strong diagonals of the cross. Christ has fallen to his knees under the weight of the huge timbers. He gazes sorrowfully out, directly at the viewer.

Stylistically, the engraving is quite close to the earliest prints by Schongauer. It includes the heavier, sketchier surfaces and linearity of all the works that are associated with his developing skill in the medium. It is a dramatic and imaginative work, created partly under the influence of a lost painting by Jan van Eyck.[14] In turn, Schongauer's engraving is reflected in works by many later artists.[15]

In this work, too, the oriental costumes and Moorish facial types among the throng surrounding Christ have been singled out as evidence that Schongauer travelled in Spain. Mainly, however, the wide range of human expression, the gestures, and the insight into behavior, reach far beyond anything that had been attempted in the medium before. All of the psychological impetus to cruelty at the event is reflected on the faces of the participants. In this respect, the print is closely related to the series of the "Passion of Christ" (L.19–30). Many of the same faces and gestures, and much of the same behavioral insight reappear in those twelve prints.

There are five versions of the Crucifixion of Christ (L.10–14). (An additional print of the same subject [L.27], in the Passion series, is discussed below.) None of the versions of the Crucifixion is simply a narrative picture of the event as chronicled in the Gospels. In each case, Christ is central, flanked by balanced groups of figures. The most elaborate is the largest (L.14). Here the mourning Virgin and John the Evangelist stand on either side of the rough-hewn log that serves as the upright of the cross. Four hovering angels catch the blood from Christ's wounds in chalices. The figure of Christ is exaggeratedly thin, particularly in his arms and legs. At the foot of the cross, which is wedged into the ground with rocks and pegs, are a skull and two bones, mortal remains of Adam whose skeleton was found, according to tradition, on the site of the Crucifixion. In back of the carefully balanced and distributed figures is a rolling, peaceful landscape. This version is usually given a rather early date. The textures and the use of line resemble features of the similarly elaborate "Life of the Virgin" series.

A second version of the Crucifixion (L.13) is nearly as large and elaborate as the previous one.

[11] As in the apse mosaic of Sta. Maria Maggiore in Rome, by Jacopo Torriti.
[12] Alan Shestack, *Fifteenth Century Engravings,* no. 75.
[13] Ms. M. 914, p. 39. The theme is traceable to the fourteenth century in both Italy and the North; see the fresco in the Dominican church at Maastricht, illustrated, for example, by P.

Clemen, *Die gotischen Monumentalmalereien der Rheinlande,* I, fig. 42, p. 37.
[14] E. Panofsky, *Early Netherlandish Painting,* I, pp. 236ff; R. A. Koch, "Martin Schongauer's 'Christ Bearing the Cross,'" *Record of the Art Museum,* Princeton University, 1955, XIV, pp. 22–30.
[15] Lehrs, *Katalog,* V, pp. 72–76.

FIGURE 14   Dutch Miniaturist, *Christ Blessing the Virgin,* miniature, ca. 1440, in the
Hours of Catherine of Cleves, The Pierpont Morgan Library, New York.

It comes closer to direct narrative illustration and bears a close resemblance to the series of Christ's Passion in figures, detail, and depiction of the event itself (L.27). Here many figures are crowded into the narrow space of the foreground against a hilly and completely barren landscape background. The cross rises from close to the bottom of the engraving all the way to the top. Christ, head bowed in death, is frontal, hanging from the rough, unplaned logs of the cross. At the left, St. John the Evangelist supports the fainting Virgin and two additional female mourners appear behind them. At the right are six soldiers, among them the sponge-bearer Stephaton. Two others on the ground gamble with him for possession of Christ's robe (John 19:23–24).

The other three representations of the Crucifixion (L.10, 11, and 12) are smaller in scale, simpler, and without landscape background. In the first, St. John the Evangelist supports the mourning Virgin at the left of the cross in a fashion similar to that in the Crucifixion discussed above (L.13). On the right are the Centurion and the spear-bearing Longinus. Both, according to various traditions, were converted at the Crucifixion. The cross is short, and the five-figured composition is quite compact. The figure of Christ is frontal and rigid; only his head is bowed in the direction of the Virgin. The other two versions of the Crucifixion (L.11 and 12) include only Christ on the cross, flanked by St. John at the right and the Virgin at the left. The first of these (L.11) is preserved in two states; in the second state there are added halos of the radiant type about the heads of each figure. It would be difficult to separate these three versions of the *Crucifixion* in the chronological development of Martin Schongauer's technique. All are products of his maturity.

THE "PASSION OF CHRIST" SERIES

The series of the "Passion of Christ," consisting of twelve sequential scenes (L.19–30), is the largest set of engravings made by Martin Schongauer. It represents the continuation, on his part, of a traditional subject-cycle for fifteenth-century engravers. Almost all of his predecessors had produced series illustrating the Passion of Christ. Schongauer's version is not only filled with the agitation, drama, and agony characteristic of German art in the fifteenth century, but he has also invested the scenes with a new and vital humanity. As in the large engraving of *Christ Carrying the Cross,* the figures are expressive of human ignorance, weakness, and cruelty.

The tormentors of Christ are not grotesque personifications of evil; they are pitiable human beings caught in the web of events and emotions. Recognizable figures appear and reappear in various scenes. The space depicted in each scene is limited but logical. Stylistically, the series appears to be a comparatively young work. The date that has been suggested for it, around 1480, probably represents the upper limit.[16]

The first scene of the series is the *Agony in the Garden* (L.19). Christ, in the middle distance, kneels in prayer. He looks upward to an angel who hovers above an outcropping rock. Three apostles, Peter, James, and John are dozing in the foreground. At the right is Judas, clutching the bag of money that he has been paid to betray Christ. He steals into the scene, followed by soldiers.

In the second print, *Christ Taken Prisoner* (L.20), Jesus is clasped and buffeted by several of the soldiers. His hands are tied, and he is led away with a rope doubled around his neck by the leader of his captors. In the foreground is St. Peter, who approaches the fallen soldier, Malchus, with dagger drawn. St. Peter's futile attempt to save Christ from capture is given prominence in the print. Judas, still clutching the money bag, departs from the scene in the opposite direction.

Next is *Christ Led Before Annas* (L.21). The leader of the captors who still clutches the rope binding Christ, Malchus with the lantern, and at least one of the other soldiers, are recognizable from the previous scene. All the figures are crowded into a simply-depicted interior space, roofed by a heavy groin-vault. In the *Flagellation of Christ* (L.22), five tormentors are distributed around the column to which Christ is bound within the narrow confines of a thick-walled room. One of the tormentors squats on the floor in the background plaiting the crown of thorns. The next print is the *Mocking of Christ* (L.23). The Lord is seated upon a low bench, dressed in a robe. He is handed a reed scepter. Pilate enters upon the scene at the left.

Sixth in the series is *Christ Before Pilate* (L.24). The enthroned governor washes his hands in water which a servant pours from a ewer into a basin. The characterization of Pilate as an effete and distracted ruler is clearly established in this scene and in the next print, the *Ecce Homo,* or *Christ Shown to the People* (L.25). In the latter engraving, Pilate weakly gestures in defense of Christ from the doorway of his palace. Beyond the figure of Christ can be seen the chamber of the Flagellation. The people gathered to condemn Christ are mostly recognizable

[16] Alan Shestack, *Fifteenth Century Engravings*, nos. 51–62.

as the tormentors from the preceding scenes. Thus the outcome of their judgment is made starkly inevitable.

The eighth print in the Passion series is the *Bearing of the Cross* (L.26). It is shown in a more restricted space than Schongauer's large engraving of the subject. The procession emerges from the city gate of Jerusalem through a passageway and under a large portcullis. In the left foreground is St. Veronica holding the sudarium with Christ's face imprinted upon it. Christ, weighed down by the heavy timbers of the cross, is at the center of the composition. The Virgin stands at the far left behind St. Veronica. At the lower right is the leader of the captors of Christ, now become chief executioner. He tugs at the rope bound around Christ's waist, while holding the nails for the crucifixion in his left hand.

The *Crucifixion* (L.27) is a centrally composed non-narrative portrayal. The cross is centered and low. Christ's figure is very elongated with short, thin arms. St. John the Evangelist is on the right and five mourning women are at the left. Past bare craggy rocks in the middle distance are the rooftops of Jerusalem and a rolling landscape. In the *Entombment* (L.28), St. John and the Virgin are in the foreground, backs to the viewer, watching as Christ's body is lowered into a huge sarcophagus by Joseph of Arimathaea and Nicodemus. Three others of the mourning women are also present. The hill of Calvary is at the right in the far distance, with the single cross of the Crucifixion atop it. Basically, however, the composition is dense and shallow, dominated by the strong horizontal of the sarcophagus. In the next scene, the *Harrowing of Hell* (L.29), the risen Christ enters from the left using his banner of victory on a cross-staff as a weapon to overthrow Satan and his demons as he liberates Adam, Eve, John the Baptist, and other worthies. The final print of the series is the *Resurrection of Christ* (L.30). The risen Christ stands in the center of the print, emerging from the open sarcophagus holding the cross-staff with its banner. Behind Christ, an angel tugs at the heavy lid of the tomb. In the foreground is the soldier Malchus, terrified by the appearance of Christ. Five other soldiers are seated or crouched around the tomb.

OTHER REPRESENTATIONS
OF CHRIST

The next four engravings in the Lehrs *Katalog*

(L.31–34) make up Schongauer's non-narrative images of Christ. The most elaborate of them is the *Man of Sorrows* (L.34). The print survives in two states. The first has the earlier form of Martin Schongauer's monogram on the face of the sill beneath the arched opening in which the scene appears. The second state has Schongauer's later monogram on the ledge of the sill. The plate has been cut down on all sides, and some of the lines have been strengthened by deeper cutting. The print shows Christ after the Crucifixion, flanked by the Virgin and St. John the Evangelist. Seven tiny mourning angels appear over their heads.

There are several versions of the theme of the Man of Sorrows in the fifteenth century. Schongauer's representation is comparatively rare as a type. It is related to the early fifteenth-century tondo by Jean Malouel, the *Trinity with the Virgin and St. John the Evangelist* in the Louvre, and to Geertgen tot Sint Jans's individualistic *Man of Sorrows* in Utrecht.[17] The engraving is one of Schongauer's earliest. Its subject is quite direct and uncomplicated. It is a votive image meant to evoke the sacrifice and sorrow of the Passion. There are numerous copies of it.

The engraving of *Christ Enthroned Between Two Angels* (L.33), which belongs to the mature years of the artist, corresponds stylistically with the engravings of *Christ Blessing the Virgin* (L.18) and the *Christ Crowning the Virgin* (L.17). Christ is seated on an immense, heavy throne, revealed by two angels who part curtains at either side of the throne. Christ wears a large crown and holds an orb and scepter in his left hand; he gestures to his right with a sign of blessing. The features of Christ are rather soft and sweet, as they are in other characteristic engravings of the period. The probability that this engraving was created as the central print in the series of "Wise and Foolish Virgins" (L.76–85) is discussed below.[18]

The other two non-narrative images of Christ are the *Infant Christ* and the *Standing Christ* (L.31–32). Each shows Christ standing frontally, gesturing in blessing with his right hand. The infant Christ, wearing a billowing cloak that leaves his body mostly nude, holds an orb in his left hand. The adult, standing Christ holds one end of a banderole that swirls over his head from the right side of the print to the left. Both of these small engravings seem to belong to the early maturity of Martin Schongauer. The engraving of the *Infant Christ* was surely inspired by a similar print by Master E.S. (L.49).

[17] Both illustrated in Panofsky, *Early Netherlandish Painting*, II, fig. 101 (Malouel), fig. 449 (Geertgen).

[18] See p. 48.

The following six engravings are Schongauer's versions of the Madonna and Child theme (L.35–40). Two of them, the *Madonna and Child with a Parrot* (L.37) and the *Madonna and Child on a Crescent* (L.40), are among the eleven earliest engravings signed with a vertically-stemmed "M" in Schongauer's monogram.

The *Madonna and Child on a Crescent* bears a close design relationship to Martin Schongauer's painting of the *Madonna and Child in a Rose Arbor* (fig. 2).[19] Iconographically, however, the engraving is far from the painted representation in Colmar. Here the Virgin is clearly associated with the Apocalyptic Woman "clothed with the sun, and the moon under her feet, and upon her head a crown of twelve stars" (Rev. 12:1). The engraving is a continuation of this popular image of the Virgin, found in paintings, sculpture, and prints throughout the later Middle Ages. Here, as in Schongauer's painting, the types of the Virgin and Child are clearly a reflection of the influence of Roger van der Weyden.

The *Madonna and Child with a Parrot* (L.37) is also stylistically close to Netherlandish works. The parallel with Dirk Bouts's *Madonna and Child at a Window* in the National Gallery, London, has been demonstrated by Alan Shestack.[20] The engraving is also closely comparable to a drawing in the Boymans-van Beuningen Museum in Rotterdam that is attributed to Roger van der Weyden.[21] It exists in two states, with several elements added to the second. The first state, in fact, is called a proof by Lehrs, since the Child holds only the stem of the pear that appears in its entirety in the second state. Also conspicuous in the second state is the added pattern on the cushion, and additional hair next to the right arm of the Virgin.

The small print of the *Madonna and Child on a Grassy Bench* (L.36) is also a fairly early work. It is comparable to the composition of the Virgin and Child in the panel painting of the *Holy Family* by Schongauer in Munich (fig. 6). The Virgin in the engraving, seated upon a grassy bench, continues the artist's use of the "Madonna of Humility" theme found in his *Madonna and Child in a Rose Arbor* in Colmar (fig. 2). The print also shows Mary holding an apple to attract the Child's attention, a traditional theme in fifteenth-century art that suggests the role of the Virgin as the "New Eve."[22]

Behind the Virgin is a wattle fence closing the Mother and Child off from a rather bleak landscape beyond. There, a river flows from the left past a bald rock-face with a few reeds at its base, on into a widening bay. At the right is a bare tree. A castle atop a hill and a few tiny ships in the bay are on the horizon of the scene.

Another version of the "Madonna of Humility" theme is the engraving of the *Madonna and Child in a Courtyard* (L.38). This print is larger in scale and begins to show the reduction in detail and geometricization of composition that characterizes Schongauer's mature engravings. Three strong vertical elements, the Virgin's head and torso, the tree, and the gate-house dominate the space. The diagonal plane of the Virgin's lap is balanced by the reclining body of the Child. The tones, however, are still created with the sketchier lines so apparent in Schongauer's earlier works. It is probable that this engraving was created at about the same time as the series of the Passion, in the artist's early maturity.

The walled isolation of Mary and the Child in this print may indicate the "hortus conclusus," one of those many epithets by which Mary is known (Song of Solomon 4:12), just as the gate may represent another Marialogical element, the "porta clausa" of Ezekiel 44:2. The clear emphasis of the print, however, is upon the Virgin and Child in a simply-represented devotional image.

The same directness characterizes the two versions of the standing Madonna, the *Madonna and Child with an Apple* (L.39) and the *Madonna and Child* (L.35). The larger of the two, the *Madonna and Child with an Apple,* is an early work, characterized by the rather heavy, somewhat irregular shading in the areas of the drapery of the Virgin's garments. The second engraving, quite tiny in scale, is harder to place in sequence, but appears by its drapery style to belong among Schongauer's mature works. Neither engraving shows any iconographic complexity nor more than the merest trace of setting. The apple held by the Child in the larger of the two engravings retains its typological meaning in reference to the "New Eve" and the "New Adam." In the smaller print the Child is empty-handed.

THE "APOSTLES" SERIES

The series of "Apostles" (L.41–52) also continues a well-established tradition among fifteenth-century printmakers. Each of Schongauer's twelve small en-

[19] See above, p. 20.

[20] Alan Shestack, *The Complete Engravings of Martin Schongauer,* New York, 1969, pp. ix, x.

[21] Panofsky, *Early Netherlandish Painting,* II, fig. 385.

[22] The concept of Mary as the "New Eve" originated in patristic writings and was widely alluded to in medieval art; for sources see Yrjö Hirn, *The Sacred Shrine,* London, 1958, pp. 205–06 notes 36–38, pp. 372–73.

gravings shows a single apostle standing against a blank background on a small hummock of earth. Stylistically they belong among the mature works, at no great distance from the small *Virgin and Child* (L.35) discussed above.

Although the attributes of the apostles vary somewhat in late medieval usage, and St. Paul may be substituted for any one of several of the twelve, it is quite apparent that the identities listed by Lehrs are correct. Here St. Paul appears in place of St. Matthias, who was elected by lot by the remaining eleven apostles in place of Judas Iscariot. Each of the figures holds his identifying attribute. Seven of them also carry books of the scriptures.[23]

SAINTS

After the "Apostles" series in the Lehrs *Katalog* are fourteen representations of male saints, numbered in alphabetical order (L.53–66). The first two are depictions of St. Anthony. The smaller (L.53) shows the saint standing frontally, a book tucked under his right arm, and holding a staff, a doubled archepiscopal cross, and a bell in his left hand. At his feet is a pig with a tiny bell in its left ear. The features and attributes of St. Anthony in this print resemble those of his portrayal on the inner right panel of the Orliac Altarpiece wings by Martin Schongauer (fig. 5).[24]

The second and larger of Schongauer's engravings of St. Anthony is the famous *Tribulations of St. Anthony* (L.54). An early work, still bearing the vertically-stemmed "M" in Schongauer's monogram, the engraving exists in two states with only minor details added to the second, as noted in the Lehrs *Katalog*.[25] The print shows the hermit St. Anthony suspended in mid-air by a vicious throng of extraordinary demons who clutch, tear, and beat upon him. At the lower right of the scene is a barren crag. Otherwise there is no landscape. The sky is indicated by an irregular pattern of horizontal dashes at the top of the engraving—one of the few instances of any attempt to indicate atmosphere in Schongauer's prints.

The engraved *Tribulations of St. Anthony* was extraordinarily influential on the work of other artists. The demons reappear in a wide variety of late fifteenth- and early sixteenth-century works of art, among the illustrations to the renowned *Nurem-*

berg Chronicle, in the "Apocalypse" series of woodcuts by Albrecht Dürer, and elsewhere. Vasari asserts that Michelangelo made a copy of the print.[26]

A small print of a *Standing Bishop* (L.55) was identified by Lehrs as "St. Augustine(?)." Bartsch, and subsequently most other scholars, have simply identified the figure as a bishop, since he carries no specific attribute. Passavant[27] suggested that the figure represented either St. Eustace or St. Hubert, and Flechsig identified him with St. Martin, patron of Colmar. In Flechsig's opinion, the *Standing Bishop* as St. Martin is paired with the small *St. Anthony* as patrons of Colmar and the neighboring monastery of Isenheim respectively.[28] If Flechsig's criteria for pairing the two on the basis of style and dimensions are applied, then the small print of the *Madonna and Child* (L.35) ought to be added to the group. Further, St. Augustine—to defend Lehrs' identification of the standing bishop—appears with St. Anthony in Nicolas von Hagenau's sculptural group in the central image of the huge Isenheim Altarpiece. At his feet in the sculpture is Jean d'Orliac, Martin Schongauer's patron, who appears at the feet of St. Anthony in the Orliac Altarpiece wings.[29]

Schongauer's engraving of the *Standing Bishop,* however, is patterned after an engraving of *St. Eligius* (L.142) by the Master E. S. and was copied in a woodcut used to depict several bishop saints among the illustrations in the *Nuremberg Chronicle.*

The engraving of *St. Christopher* (L.56) is an early print, made before 1476 according to Lehrs.[30] Baum and Flechsig both list the print as a late work, but Shestack has demonstrated stylistic support for Lehrs's early dating.[31]

Holding his voluminous cloak above the water, the saint wades from right to left across a wide, placid river carrying the Christ-child on his back and a huge staff in his right hand. On the shore in the left middle distance is the hermit of the legend. A blossoming flag (*Iris pseudacorus*), a characteristic plant of marshy ground or river banks, appears in the right foreground. The composition is direct and simple, and the image corresponds to the traditional portrayal of this popular saint.

Schongauer made two engravings of St. George, both showing him in combat with the dragon. The larger of the two (L. 58) is one of the eleven earliest prints by the artist, signed with the vertically-stemmed "M" in Schongauer's monogram. The en-

[23] For the Apostles and their attributes see C. Minott, "The St. Matthew Page in the 'Hours of Catherine of Cleves,'" *North Carolina Museum of Art Bulletin,* IX, 1970, pp. 68–73.
[24] See pp. 20–22 above.
[25] Lehrs, *Katalog,* V, p. 244.
[26] G. Vasari, *Vite,* ed. Milanesi, V, pp. 395ff.

[27] J. D. Passavant, *Le peintre-graveur,* II, Leipzig, 1860, p. 112.
[28] Flechsig, *Schongauer,* pp. 236–38.
[29] See above, p. 20 footnote 11.
[30] Lehrs, *Katalog,* V, pp. 253–54.
[31] See Alan Shestack, *Fifteenth Century Engravings,* no. 81.

FIGURE 15   Albrecht Dürer, *Terence Writing His Comedies,* preparatory drawing for
woodcut, 1492, Oeffentliche Kunstsammlung, Basel.

graving is circular in format, though printed from
a square plate. It shows St. George mounted, at-
tacking the dragon with upraised sword. The
dragon, already transfixed by the saint's broken
lance, cringes at the left by the mouth of a cave. In
the middle distance kneels the princess Theodolinda,
and far behind her, on a parapet of her castle atop
a rock crag, are her parents. The dragon's body has
been adapted from the same type of lizard as that
of the demon who clutches the left shoulder and
thigh of St. Anthony in the large print of the
Tribulations of St. Anthony (L.54).

The other engraving of *St. George Fighting the
Dragon* (L.57) is one of Schongauer's tiniest. The
saint, astride his caparisoned mount, and wearing
armor and a plumed helmet, attacks the dragon with
a long lance. The monster has fallen backward. In
the background is the princess, kneeling with clasped
hands, watching the combat. The engraving, probably a mature work, has been reduced to the essen-
tial, traditional elements of the story.

St. John the Baptist (L.59) is one of several figures of saints, male and female, engraved in large
scale against a plain background and standing on a
rounded hummock of bare or grassy earth. They are
all slightly different in measurement, and probably
do not represent a specific series. Each is accompanied by traditional, identifying attributes. St. John
the Baptist wears animal-pelt garments under a
shapeless robe. He carries a book on which is re-
posing the "Lamb of God," St. John's own epithet

for Christ (John 1:29). The lamb holds the pennant inscribed with a cross, symbol of the victorious
Christ. Stylistically, the engraving belongs to the
works of Schongauer's early maturity.

St. John on Patmos (L.60) is an engraving of St.
John the Evangelist seated in a landscape and com-
posing his Apocalypse. The Virgin and Child, as
described in the vision of St. John, appear to the
saint in the sky. The print is clearly a refinement of
the version of the scene by the Master E.S. (L.151).
Lehrs lists several copies of the whole print and of
details in other works. It was just as clearly an influence on the young Albrecht Dürer, who modified
the composition but retained its spirit in his preparatory drawing for the woodcut of *Terence Writing
His Comedies,* done in Basel in 1492 (fig. 15).

The engraving of *St. John on Patmos* is one of the
few, mostly early works in which recognizable plants
grow in the foreground. St. John's symbol as one of
the evangelists is the eagle. The bird, more heraldic
than ornithological, stands in front of the saint. The
Virgin, standing, on the moon, arrayed with the sun's
radiance, and crowned with twelve stars, corresponds to St. John's vision of the Apocalyptic
Woman (Rev. 12:1). Schongauer used the same attributes for the Virgin in his engraving of the
Madonna on a Crescent (L.40).

The engraving of *St. Lawrence* (L.61) is a direct
portrayal of the early Christian deacon and martyr,
standing in tunic and dalmatic. The saint holds a
book in his right hand and the iron grille of his

martyrdom and martyr's palm-branch in his left. According to most scholars this print is one of Schongauer's last. It may have been intended as one of a pair, the other being *St. Stephen* (L.66), which has almost exactly the same dimensions. Both saints were engraved in the late style of Martin Schongauer; both stand against a completely blank background with a single, horizontal floor-line behind them.

The engraving of *St. Martin* (L.62) is a fairly early print. It shows the saint on a hummock of earth in the act of dividing his cloak for a beggar who crouches in the lower right corner of the scene. The simple monumentality of the composition in this engraving of Schongauer's name-saint is close to that of the equally early engraving, *St. John the Baptist* (L.59).

Schongauer's *St. Michael* (L.63), in the artist's mature style, shows the archangel standing triumphant over the Satanic dragon, thrusting a spear into the open, gasping mouth of the monster. The demon, writhing but powerless, grasps the spear in futile self-defense. The subject is traditional, derived from the Apocalypse (Rev. 12:7–9); however, Schongauer has made a significant change in the traditional representation. St. Michael is usually depicted as a warrior in armor, at least when battling the dragon. The two engravings of *St. Michael* (L.153 and 154) by the Master E.S. are typical. But Schongauer's *St. Michael* wears a long alb or tunic with a flowing cape over it, fastened at the breast by a morse. This garb, and the general form of the archangel, seem to derive from the figure of St. Michael weighing souls in Roger van der Weyden's famous *Last Judgment* Altarpiece in Beaune. There is no doubt that Schongauer's engraving, in turn, had a profound influence on the woodcut of the *War in Heaven* (B.72) in the "Apocalypse" series by Albrecht Dürer.[32]

The larger of Schongauer's two engravings of *St. Sebastian* (L.65) is very close in dimensions and style to the engravings of *St. John on Patmos* (L. 60) and *St. Christopher* (L.56). Each shows the saint in a somewhat simplified and formalized landscape. This engraving shows St. Sebastian bound to a tree, his hands over his head, and his arms, legs, and torso transfixed by many arrows. None of his tormentors is shown. The landscape is barren, with no detail save the dry, truncated tree to which the saint is bound and a few blades of grass at his feet.

The other engraving of *St. Sebastian* (L.64) is the smallest of all Martin Schongauer's prints. The saint's hands are tied separately above his head to a tall tree-stump, and he stands on a grassy hum-

mock. The print is probably from Schongauer's early maturity.

The tonsured *St. Stephen* (L.66) shows the early deacon and martyr standing and holding the martyr's palm in his right hand. He holds the rocks of his death by lapidation gathered in his dalmatic. It has already been noted, above and elsewhere, that the *St. Stephen* was probably intended to be paired with the engraving of *St. Lawrence* (L.61). Both prints are very late in Schongauer's stylistic development. Perhaps they can be dated after 1489, for St. Stephen is the patron of the Münster in Breisach wherein the artist was engaged in painting the huge *Last Judgment* fresco.

The following five engravings in the Lehrs *Katalog* (L.67–71) are the single figures of female saints, all composed with the same simplicity and directness as the majority of the male saints. *St. Agnes* (L.67) is alphabetically and probably chronologically the first of the group. She stands against an unadorned background on a grassy knoll holding a book and a martyr's palm-branch with her symbol, the figure of a lamb, at her feet. The print is an early work, probably contemporary with the figure of *John the Baptist* (L.59).

St. Barbara (L.68) is a small scale engraving, clearly one of a pair with the small *St. Catherine* (L.69). Both saints are crowned and both appear with their major attributes. Stylistically, they belong to the developed, mature works. Both are particularly venerated saints, virgin princesses martyred for their faith. There is no reason to suppose that they are part of an unexecuted, larger series.[33]

St. Barbara reads from a breviary. The tower, symbol of her ordeal of faith, is at her feet. Beyond her is a vaguely indicated landscape.

St. Catherine stands on a grassy knoll, holding a book and the sword of her martyrdom. At her feet is a fragment of a blade-studded wheel, part of the engine devised by the Emperor of Alexandria to torture her. She was saved by the intervention of an angel only to suffer death by decapitation, hence the sword.

A second, larger engraving of *St. Catherine* (L.70) was made by Martin Schongauer. It is iconographically identical to the small version except that in the larger example St. Catherine does not hold a book. Stylistically, the larger print seems earlier than the paired *St. Barbara* and *St. Catherine*.

St. Veronica (L.71) is a small engraving of the female saint who wiped the sweat from Christ's face as he bore the cross to Calvary. Miraculously, the kerchief took the imprint of Christ's face. In the

[32] Illustrated, for example, in E. Panofsky, *Albrecht Dürer*, 2nd ed., Princeton, 1945, II, fig. 81.

[33] Alan Shestack, *Fifteenth Century Engravings*, nos. 85, 86.

print St. Veronica holds the large sudarium in front of her, displaying the facial imprint of Christ. It is characteristic of the period that the sacred relic shown is far larger than the natural scale of the saint.

Many of the early engravers made representations of St. Veronica with the sudarium, or of the sudarium alone. She is pictured in the *Bearing of the Cross* (L.26) in the Passion series by Schongauer. While painted representations of St. Veronica, especially in Germany, are not particularly rare, it may well be that the printmaker felt particular sympathy for the transferred image. Schongauer's print is usually placed among the mature works by the artist, although the robust face of Christ is similar to his earlier representations rather than to the more slender, gentler features of Christ in the mature works.

THE FOUR EVANGELISTS' SYMBOLS

The following fifteen engravings listed in the Lehrs *Katalog* are grouped under the heading "*Religiöses*," that is, symbolic or allegorical images with Christian meaning. The first four (L.72–75) consist of a set of the symbolic figures of the evangelists. Each is circular, printed from a square plate of dimensions similar to the round *St. George* (L.58). But the evangelists' symbols, the traditional winged "beasts," adapted from the vision of Ezekiel and the Apocalypse and identified with the evangelists since the early Christian era, are late works, probably among the last produced by Schongauer. Each is nimbed, and a ribbon of banderole traverses the design of each plate.

St. Matthew (L.72) is represented as a winged man, often understandably called an angel. The kneeling figure with wings outstretched is beautifully worked into the circular design. Since Matthew's Gospel opens with the human genealogy of Christ, his is the human symbol of the Biblical visions. St. Mark (L.73) is symbolized by a lion, also winged. Mark's Gospel opens with "the voice of one crying in the wilderness . . . ," an image best suited to the lion of the vision. Schongauer's lion is seen in profile, facing left. The symbol of St. Luke (L.74) is an ox, since Luke's Gospel dwells on Christ's priesthood, and the ox is a venerable symbol of priestly sacrifice. In Schongauer's version the winged ox is young, thin, and bony, with a head nearly identical to that of the ox in the early *Nativity* (L.5). The eagle, an ancient symbol of divine inspiration, was chosen to represent St. John the Evangelist, whose Gospel is most concerned with the revelation of

Christ's divine nature. Schongauer's print of the *Eagle of St. John* (L.75) shows a stern and strong eagle very similar to the one in his engraving of *St. John on Patmos* (L.60).

THE WISE AND FOOLISH VIRGINS

The *Five Wise Virgins* (L.76–80) and the *Five Foolish Virgins* (L.81–85) also form a series—two interdependent sets of engravings. These elegantly dressed ladies are all among the late works by Martin Schongauer. The two processions face each other, the wise virgins each bearing lighted lamps and wearing a leafy, festive crown on the left, the foolish on the right. The foolish virgins' lamps are empty and all are held inverted; their crowns have fallen to the ground. All are downcast, and two weep outright. Together, of course, the series is an illustration of one of Christ's parables, a complex if vivid allegory of salvation on the Day of Judgment (Matt. 25:1–13).

It may be that the two "leaders" of the processions of wise and foolish virgins (L.80 and 81), who are in profile, were intended to appear as in discourse. The moment at which the foolish virgins asked to buy oil from the wise ones would be appropriate. Nonetheless, a more probable hypothesis is that the engraving of *Christ Enthroned Between Two Angels* (L.33) was created as the central image between the two processions. The engraving is larger, but the figures are in proportion and the rectangular format is also proportional. Christ gestures significantly to his right, and the angels' actions fit the scheme. The angel on the left pulls the curtain back, revealing Christ and his throne. The angel on the right pulls the curtain forward, closing off the view of Christ from those approaching at the right. His gaze in that direction is explicable as a response to the five foolish virgins approaching from that side.

The engraving *A Foolish Virgin* (L.86) is a problematic print. The figure is frontal, in half-length, holding an inverted oil-lamp. The plate seems to have been cropped at least at the bottom, and the lower part and left arm, in contrast to the upper part of the plate, seem to have been sketched in rather summarily. It has been suggested by Lehrs and others that Schongauer left this plate unfinished and that it was completed by one of his close followers. Ostensibly, the left arm of the figure is held to be weak in contour and uncharacteristic of the artist. Shestack agrees with the theory that this work was an unfinished one, completed by a second artist.[34] He rightly points out that the style of the work is early rather than late. The turban worn by the foolish virgin has also caused speculation. Flechsig, who argues that the work is entirely Schongauer's, goes on to interpret the figure as a Moorish woman drawn by Schongauer in Spain and later committed to engraving with an inverted lamp as symbol of her heathen state.[35]

Flechsig has rightly observed that the *Foolish Virgin* represents the largest figure ever done by Martin Schongauer in an engraving. The matter of scale is important to many of the additional arguments about the print. The print which is closest in scale to the *Foolish Virgin* is the print of the *Man of Sorrows* (L.34), an early print, the plate for which was later reworked and cropped. A comparison of contours, for instance those of Christ's left arm and the drawing of the hands, ought to demonstrate sufficiently that the *Foolish Virgin* is entirely Schongauer's own work. If the lines, particularly in the garments of the figure, seem somewhat bolder and without the refinements of hatchure and delicate shading, the overall effect contributes to the uncircumspect young lady's dishevelment. A summary glance through Flemish and German painting in the fifteenth century ought to dispel any interpretation of a turban as an indication of direct oriental or Moorish experience. The rather raw-boned, large features of the girl, fit Schongauer's style well. They are even similar to those of the Virgin in the *Madonna and Child in a Rose Arbor* of 1473 (fig. 2).

SECULAR SUBJECTS

Eight of Martin Schongauer's engravings were catalogued by Lehrs under the heading of "Profanes." The *Fighting Apprentices* (L.87) is a tiny print showing two youths in a corner wrestling and pulling hair. One youth menaces the other with a pair of tongs. At the right of the print is a crucible on a three-legged stand and a bellows; a cap has been scuffed into the corner at the left. The print shows a directly observed flareup of youthful tempers, usually cited as evidence that Schongauer was familiar with the workshop environment of the goldsmith, although nothing specifically limits the *mise en scène* to a goldsmith's shop.

The *Miller* (L.88) simply depicts a laborer with a flour sifter tucked under one arm driving a laden donkey accompanied by its foal. There is no landscape except for a single grassy ground-line. The

Two Moors in Conversation (L.89) shows two men in semi-fanciful oriental dress, walking to the left and engaged in conversation. The nearer wears a sort of turban and has a curved dagger ornamented with a crescent. He and his companion, who grips the hilt of a curved, sheathed sword, both wear short tunics and turned boots.

The largest and most interesting of the secular prints by Martin Schongauer is the early engraving of a *Peasant Family Going to Market* (L.90). A coarse and shabbily dressed man, the father of the family, is at the left. He is burdened with a sack of vegetables, a basket of eggs, a battered sword, and the reins of a thin, tangled-maned horse which bears his wife and child along the road. Beyond is a detailed landscape, characteristic of the early Schongauer prints, with a village church, a well, farm buildings, and other figures straggling along the road to the market. The print is nearly square, and it is signed with the vertically-stemmed "M" of Schongauer's early form of monogram.

Four of the secular engravings are of various animals. The *Family of Pigs* (L.91) shows simply a boar and a sow with five piglets. The *Deer and Doe* (L.92) is also a direct representation of the two animals. A similar pair are visible in the background of Schongauer's *Flight into Egypt* (L.7). Both of these animal prints are small, horizontally rectangular scenes, each with a simple ground-line to establish the setting. The *Griffin* (L.93) and the *Elephant* (L.94) are larger prints. The former is a highly individualized representation of the creature of mythology. Instead of an eagle's head and lion's body, Schongauer's griffin has the head of some rapacious bird with fangs and lappet ears, fierce-taloned forelegs, and the body, tail, and cloven-hooved hind legs of an ox. Unappealing as this combination of features may seem, the monster is heroically designed in the square space of the plate. The *Elephant* is only slightly closer to zoological reality. His immensity is emphasized by the two tiny faces of soldiers peering out through the crenellations at the top of a basket-weave howdah strapped to the back of the beast. The engraving manages to convey the impression of the anatomical enormity of an elephant, if not its physical contours. Flechsig has been able to trace evidence of an actual elephant brought through southern Germany in 1483.[36] Perhaps the presence of such a rare beast inspired Martin Schongauer's print. His brother, Ludwig Schongauer, also made a print of an elephant (L.4).[37] Ludwig's inspiration has nothing to do with Martin Schongauer's *Elephant*, however. Rather, it

[34] Alan Shestack, *Fifteenth Century Engravings*, no. 105.
[35] Flechsig, *Schongauer*, pp. 203–06.

[36] Flechsig, *Schongauer*, pp. 75–79.
[37] Flechsig, *Schongauer*, pl. 4, facing p. 72.

is a fattened version of the ox in his brother's symbol of St. Luke (L.74), wearing an elephant mask.

In his mature years, Martin Schongauer produced a series of ten engravings of coats-of-arms (L.95–104). Each print is circular, printed from a square plate, and all are nearly identical in size. The shields in each are held by an assortment of figures —an angel, a peasant, three ladies, a Turk, three wild men, and a wild woman with a child. Most of the arms are traceable to families of the burgher class of fifteenth-century Germany. It seems doubtful, as Flechsig has observed, that these prints were made as goldsmith's models, which is the traditional interpretation,[38] although the art of engraving coats-of-arms, well-established among Schongauer's predecessors, is surely an inheritance from the goldsmith and artisan shops where engraving began.

The *Bishop's Crosier* (L.105) is the first of two engravings listed by Lehrs in the category of *"Geräte"* ("utensils"). The print is a detailed representation of an ornately designed bishop's staff. It is signed with Schongauer's monogram, the early form of which appears like a tiny maker's mark, on the shaft of the staff just below an ornamental ferrule. In the circular center of the crook, at the top of the staff, is the enthroned, crowned Virgin holding the standing Christ-child in her lap. At either side of the Virgin's ornate throne is a music-making angel. At the upper end of the staff is a decorative series of niches surrounding its eight or nine sides. In the three niches facing the viewer are statuettes of saints. At the left is St. Margaret with a tiny cross-staff implanted in the mouth of a dragon at her feet. In the center is a Christian emperor with orb and scepter, and at the right is St. Barbara with a chalice and sword.

The composition of the enthroned Virgin and Child with angels is clearly influenced by prints of the subject by the Master E.S. The work is surely not a pattern-design for a goldsmith's use. Nonetheless, it shows Martin Schongauer's clear respect for the artisan's creation and his knowledge of the best of that craft.

The same can be said for the *Censer* (L.106). This implement, also remarkably ornate, is represented in a large-scale print and is probably also a comparatively early work. The closest relative of these two utensils among Schongauer's pictorial work in prints is the candlestick at the foot of the Virgin's bed in the *Death of the Virgin* (L.16).

The only figures in the censer are angels. Only eight of the twelve implied by the design pattern are visible. An extensive ornamental pattern of grapevines, scrollwork, tracery, and leaf-crockets embellishes the rest of its surface. The large scale and close view of the censer exaggerates perspectival distortion of the base and ground-plane on which the censer rests. But the cast shadows and the overall intricacy of detail emphasize the artist's fascination for the metal-worker's craft.

Finally, Lehrs attributes to Martin Schongauer nine ornament prints (L.107–115). These, too, demonstrate Schongauer's interest in the decorative aspect of late Gothic tradition and the continuation of a form of engraving practiced by nearly all fifteenth-century practitioners of the art. They may be intended as artisan's models—almost certainly they were used as such—but each manages to convey a sense of internal design as well. They represent intricate scroll-work, leaves, tendrils, flowers, and occasional berries. In the midst of all are occasional birds —storks, herons, parrots, an owl, and smaller fowl. There is a range of complexity and size among the prints in this group, but no indication of their place in the development of Schongauer's style or, as far as can be deemed here, no iconographic enlightenment.

ST. JAMES AT THE BATTLE OF CLAVIJO

The final pages of the fifth volume of the Lehrs *Katalog* are devoted to a section he called "Engravings with Schongauer's monogram by other hands." This appendix first lists the prints in the Bartsch and Passavant catalogues no longer accepted as being by the artist. Then, in the single full catalogue entry under this heading, is entered the large engraving of *St. James at the Battle of Clavijo* (fig. 16). While it is predominantly accepted today as an authentic work by Martin Schongauer, this print may still be called controversial. It shows a miracle of St. James, his rallying of the army of Ramiro I, Christian king of Spain, against the forces of Abd-er-Rahman the Moor, or at least one of the thirty-eight occasions listed in Spanish history when the saint appeared in the midst of a battle to encourage the Christians on to victory over the heathen Moors.

The print is nearly exactly the same size as the great *Christ Carrying the Cross* (L.9). It is stylistically very close to that print as well, although probably slightly earlier. But it was never finished. For some reason, Martin Schongauer brought the print very nearly to completion and then abandoned it. The most obvious lacuna appears in the hind-

---

[38] Flechsig, *Schongauer*, pp. 81–86.

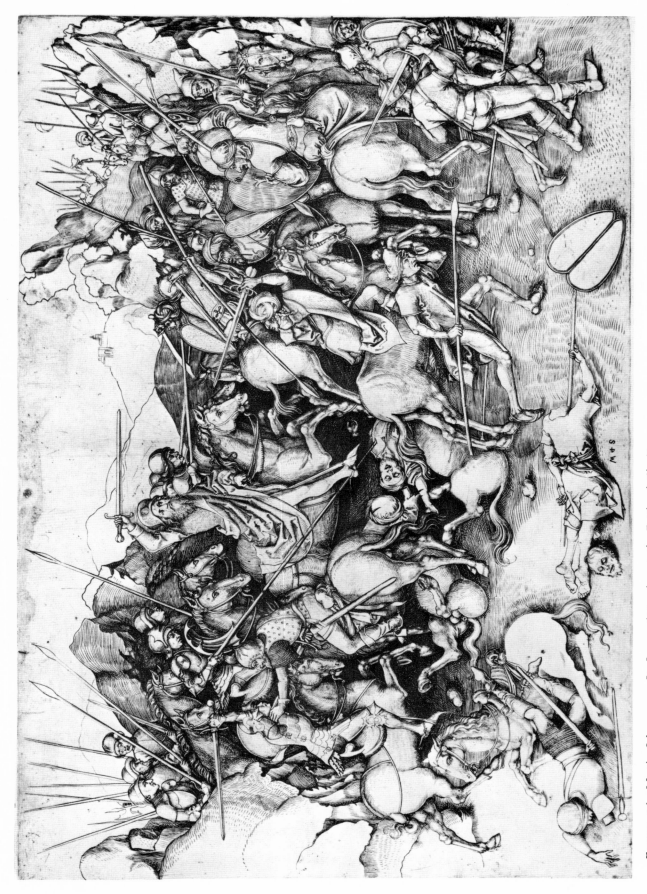

FIGURE 16 Martin Schongauer, *St. James Appearing at the Battle of Clavijo*, engraving, ca. 1475, National Gallery of Art, The Rosenwald Collection, Jenkintown.

quarters of the fallen horse in the left foreground. The longest discussion of this print, providing convincing reasons for its attribution to Schongauer, is that by Flechsig.[39]

The subject of the print is not particularly familiar outside of Spanish art. That, and the early date to which it stylistically belongs, are further arguments for the artist's presumed youthful journey to Spain.

The arguments against identifying the engraving of *St. James at the Battle of Clavijo* as an authentic work by Martin Schongauer, presented by Max Lehrs and others, are not convincing.[40] The print is not particularly well composed or organized, which must be the very reason why Schongauer abandoned it before completion. But the faces, costumes, and details are clearly Schongauer's own work.[41]

[39] Flechsig, *Schongauer,* pp. 253–82.

[40] Max Lehrs first expressed his doubts of the print's authenticity in an article, "Der deutsche und niederländische Kupferstich des 15 Jahrhunderts in den kleineren Sammlungen," *Repertorium für Kunstwissenschaft,* XV, 1892, pp. 130ff, 161.

[41] See further, the discussion in Alan Shestack, *Fifteenth Century Engravings,* no. 42.

Conclusion

MARTIN Schongauer's art never suffered obscurity. He was famed and successful in his own lifetime and exerted a powerful influence on succeeding generations, not only in Germany, but in all northern Europe and even in Italy. To analyze his art critically it is necessary to focus on the phases of transition in fifteenth-century painting and graphic arts. Many of Schongauer's prints seem to be refinements of works by earlier printmakers, particularly those of the Master E.S.—refinements that utilize the style of earlier painters' works, particularly that of Roger van der Weyden. Thus, in scholarly interpretation, Martin Schongauer rather consistently emerges as something of a conservative, primarily transitional artist in the development of German art, a successor to such men as Stefan Lochner, Konrad Witz, and the Master E.S., and a harbinger of the emerging German masters of the early sixteenth century—Albrecht Dürer, Matthias Grünewald, Albrecht Altdorfer, and their contemporaries.

It is inevitable that Schongauer, because of his transitional position, has been accorded less credit as an innovator than he deserves. His art is far less complex than that of the elaborate symbol-world depicted by the major Netherlandish painters in the middle third of the century, even though his style is partly evolved from theirs. Particularly in the mature works, he has concentrated his scenes, giving them a subdued visual clarity and unprecedented directness. In this, his art contrasts, too, with the pictorial exuberance of his German predecessors and successors.

Further, his work is still completely free of the innovation and style of the Italian Renaissance and far from the esoteric advances of scholarly humanism. But there is a compassionate human understanding in Schongauer's works that outweighs the somewhat saccharine features and the occasional monotony of detail. His works have an openness of composition and a freedom of gesture and expression that draws attention without agitation. There is a likeness of purpose, despite Schongauer's late Gothic style, to some of the best Florentines of his own day. Max Geisberg's reference to the *Madonna and Child in a Rose Arbor* as the "German Sistine Madonna" is not a wholly unwarranted comparison.[1]

Geisberg's discussion of Martin Schongauer includes the most complete bibliographical data since the Lehrs *Katalog,* adding material up to 1935. Because it is an entry in the *Künstlerlexicon,* however, the work contains only a summary study of Martin Schongauer. There is a short biography, a commentary on his art, and a listing of the works. In his article, Geisberg follows the hypothesis that Schongauer was born in Colmar about 1430. He conjectures that the artist was primarily active as a goldsmith until the late 1460's. Thus Albrecht Dürer's assertion that Schongauer was a "jung gsell" in 1470, is interpreted as indication that he had just begun as a painter and engraver at that time.[2]

The engravings that represent elaborate goldsmithery, the *Bishop's Crozier* (L.105), the *Censer* (L.106), the candlestick in the *Death of the Virgin* (L.16), plus the pattern-designs in the ornament prints (L.107–115) and the depiction of the (goldsmith's?) *Apprentices Fighting* (L.87), are cited by Geisberg as evidence of first-hand experience in the craft. But Martin Schongauer's father and at least two of his brothers were goldsmiths. Through them he would surely have gained intimate familiarity and honest respect for their artisanry. The engravings have little technical value for the goldsmith.

Geisberg accepts the date on Martin Schongauer's portrait in Munich (fig. 1) as 1453, without questioning the epithet "Hipsch Martin Schongauer Maler" at least fifteen years before he took up painting. If the inscription was added or copied by Hans Burgkmair after his apprenticeship with Schongauer in 1488, the date is more apt to be 1483, since Burgkmair's drawing in Vienna establishes his use of an "S" for the figure 8.[3]

The theory that Martin Schongauer was born

[1] Max Geisberg, "Martin Schongauer," entry in Thieme-Becker, *Künstlerlexikon,* XXX, 1936, pp. 249–54, especially p. 251.

[2] Geisberg, pp. 249–50; see p. 14 above.
[3] See footnote 13, p. 14.

around 1430 had been advanced by several scholars just prior to Geisberg's study.[4] Several new attributions of panel paintings, made by Ernst Buchner and others more or less to fit a hypothetical earlier style, are listed by Geisberg, albeit with doubts. Then in 1941 Buchner published his monograph on the paintings of Martin Schongauer.[5] Buchner discussed four paintings as early works. Among these, only one, the *Madonna and Child in a Chamber* in Basel (fig. 9), has been generally accepted as an authentic work.[6]

Buchner devoted a chapter to the influence of Roger van der Weyden, assuming that for a period before 1465 Schongauer worked in Roger's workshop or in the "vicinity" of the great Brussels master. Buchner's comparisons of features, gestures, and artistic spirit between the two artists make a reasonable claim to Schongauer's familiarity with paintings by Roger van der Weyden. These comparisons figure prominently in his discussion of the major Schongauer paintings: the *Madonna and Child in a Rose Arbor,* the Orliac Altarpiece wings, the panels in Munich, Berlin, and Vienna, and the Breisach fresco. Buchner's book, too, contains a valuable bibliography for the individual paintings in a comprehensive *Werkverzeichnis* ("catalogue") appended to the monograph.

Eduard Flechsig's monograph on Martin Schongauer, though mostly completed in 1944, did not finally reach publication until 1951. The book is an important and basic contribution to our present interpretation of Schongauer's life despite its tendency to polemics. Flechsig, who died before his book reached publication and therefore could not govern its final editing, presents the best arguments in behalf of many controversial views. His treatment of the Munich portrait of Schongauer and its inscriptions is convincing, if over-emphatic, as is his argument for acceptance of the engraving of *St. James at the Battle of Clavijo.* Other aspects of his analysis of the artist have met with less success, however, such as the use of the direction of light-source as a criterion for the chronology of the engravings. Nonetheless, with Flechsig's study of Schongauer, the weight of evidence shifted in support of the later birth-date for the artist.[7]

Concurrent with Flechsig's work, Julius Baum's monograph on the artist was published in Vienna in 1948. Baum's scholarly conclusions, frequently parallel to those of Flechsig, are presented succinctly and are supplemented by listings of the documents, by fairly thorough footnotes and by a useful, complete set of illustrations.

In the catalogue of the exhibition of fifteenth-century engravings in the National Gallery of Art collection, held in Washington in 1967–68, Alan Shestack presented an excellent short summary of the artist, as well as a scholarly interpretation of his career.[8] Further observations, particularly on the artist's technique, were made by Shestack in a brief introduction to Schongauer's prints for a recent paperbound publication.[9]

In sum, Martin Schongauer's art can now be recognized in its individuality and accepted on its own merits. The hypothesis that it was he who introduced Netherlandish advances in Germany or specifically in the Upper Rhine area is no longer defensible. The Netherlandish masters clearly exerted their influence on Stefan Lochner, the Master E.S., and even Schongauer's presumptive teacher, Caspar Isenmann. No longer is it necessary to assume that Schongauer worked in Roger van der Weyden's shop in order to learn his style, or that he was a pupil of Master E.S. in engraving. The overwhelming influence of both was inescapable. But the reduction and simplification that progress through Schongauer's works, the emphasis on pure form, and the drama with which the events are represented, constitute a different trend from those of his Flemish and German predecessors.

In other respects Martin Schongauer remains an "artist's artist," best appreciated by practitioners of the difficult art of engraving. His technical advances in the representation of light and shadow, tones, and nearly-sculptural form constituted a major gift to succeeding generations of printmakers. No longer was the art two-dimensional and outlinear. Albrecht Dürer, above all, recognized this aspect of Schongauer's art, and immeasurably furthered the process of refinement on just these technical bases. Dürer acknowledged his debt to Schongauer frequently, in unconcealed, redintegrative use of figures, themes, and whole compositions "im zu eren." Just so did Schongauer honor Roger van der Weyden and the Master E.S.

---

[4] E. Buchner, "Augsburger Kunst der Spätgotik und Renaissance," *Beiträge zur Geschichte der deutschen Kunst,* II, 1928, pp. 16ff; K. Bauch, "Schongauers Frühwerke," *Oberrheinische Kunst,* V, 1932, pp. 171ff.
[5] E. Buchner, *Martin Schongauer als Maler,* Berlin, 1941.
[6] See p. 28 above, for doubts on this painting, too.

[7] But see A. Stange, *Deutsche Malerei der Gotik,* Berlin, 1955, VII, pp. 17–24. Stange maintains the view that Schongauer was born about 1435.
[8] Alan Shestack, *Fifteenth Century Engravings,* nos. 34–115.
[9] Alan Shestack, *The Complete Engravings of Martin Schongauer,* New York, 1969.

Plates

Plates

The following section presents Martin Schongauer's prints, arranged in the numerical sequence followed by Lehrs in his *Geschichte und Kritischer Katalog*. In some cases two states of a print are illustrated, distinguished by roman numerals.

1

2

3

4

5

6

7

8

10

11.I

11.II

12

13

14

15

16.I

16.II

17

18

19

20

21

22

23

24

25

26

27

28

29

30

31

32

33

34.I

M ✝ S

34.II

35

36

37.I

37.II

38

39

40

41

42

43

44

45

46

47

48

49

50

51

52

53

M✝S

54.I

54.II

55

56

57

58

59

60

61

62

63

64

65

66

67

68

69

70

71

72

73

74

75

76

77

78

79

80

81

82

83

84

85

86

87

88

89

90

91

92

93

94

95

96

97

98

99

100

101

102

103

104

105

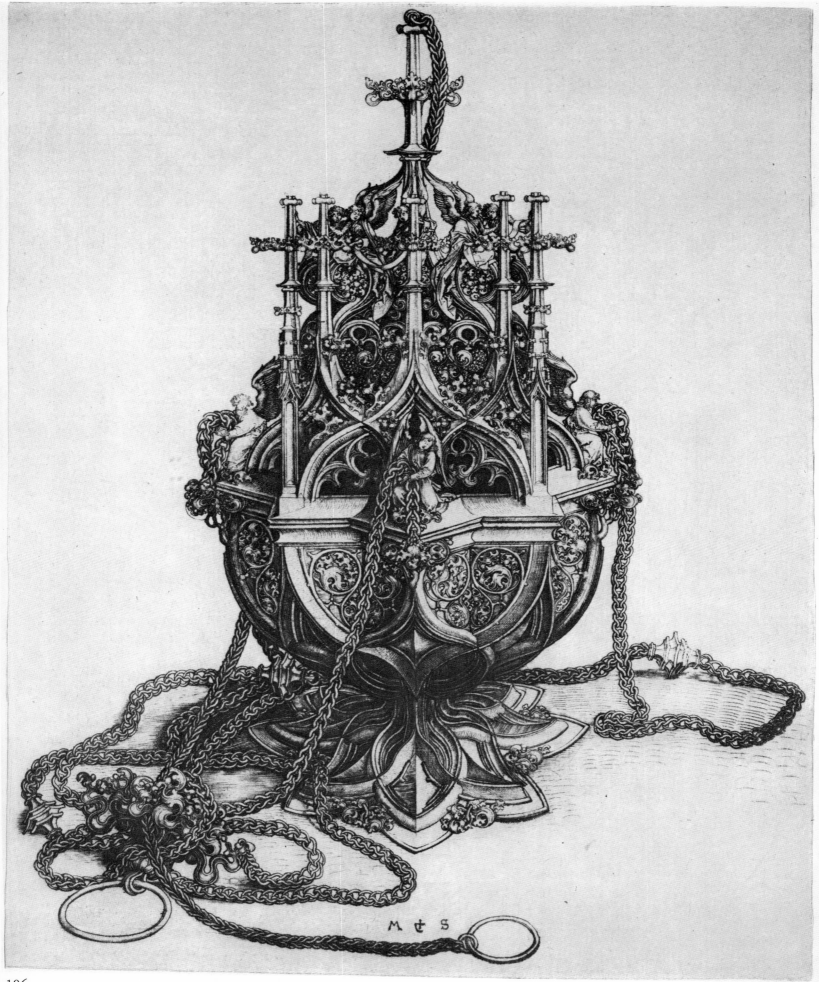

106

107

108

109

110

111

112

113

114

115

Index

Index